清代雕母研究

黄思贤 著

沈阳出版发行集团
沈阳出版社

图书在版编目（CIP）数据

清代雕母研究 / 黄思贤著 . -- 沈阳：沈阳出版社，
2020.11
　ISBN 978-7-5716-1209-2

　Ⅰ . ①清… Ⅱ . ①黄… Ⅲ . ①古钱（考古）—研究—中
国—清代 Ⅳ . ① K875.64

　中国版本图书馆 CIP 数据核字 (2020) 第 154668 号

出版发行：沈阳出版发行集团 | 沈阳出版社
　　　　　（地址：沈阳市沈河区南翰林路 10 号　邮编：110011）
网　　址：http://www.sycbs.com
印　　刷：武汉市金港彩印有限公司
幅面尺寸：210mm×285mm
印　　张：15
字　　数：140 千字
出版时间：2020 年 11 月第 1 版
印刷时间：2020 年 11 月第 1 次印刷
责任编辑：战婷婷
封面设计：树上微出版
版式设计：树上微出版
责任校对：张　娜
责任监印：杨　旭

书　　号：ISBN 978-7-5716-1209-2
定　　价：298.00 元

联系电话：024-24112447 024-62564951
E－mail：sy24112447@163.com

本书若有印装质量问题，影响阅读，请与出版社联系调换。

自序

　　我的前半生有喜有愁。童年生长在中国的农村，因为家境问题，转换了无数次中小学，所以有关中国文化、中国语言的根基都打得不好。后来到了香港，进入皇仁书院学习了二年，不久便移居美国了。

　　一九五八年十二月到达美国加利福尼亚州，一九五九年定居洛杉矶一直到现在。

　　一九六○年就读于美国加州大学（UCLA），一九六四年取得学士学位，一九六八年取得南加州大学（USC）博士学位，一九六八至一九六九年在加州大学做博士后研究，一九七六年取得加州大学（UCLA）医学博士学位。

　　从一九六二年至一九八四年，从事多项研究。从基础光学到激光，从液晶电视到平面电视，后来又进行超导（电）性的研究。

　　一九七八年我开始在洛杉矶市行医，并兼任医院和保健公司的管理工作。本着行医济世、回馈社会的宗旨，十多年前在中国上海开设了一家中美合资医院。

　　一九六七年与郑氏结婚，育有一子一女，可惜郑氏不幸在一九九三年逝世。

　　现与林女士共结连理，生活美满，事业尚算顺利，是人生的第二个开端。

　　我的古钱收藏已有四十年的历史，起初只是在美国各中国城、古玩铺买些普通品，三十多年前从 E. Kann 先生的藏品中买了十数枚元宝，后来从 Howard Gibbs 藏品，买了一些空首布和金错刀。一个偶然的机会又收购了罗彻斯特大学所藏 Speicher 氏的所有收藏品。这是我收藏古钱的开始。

　　上世纪七十和八十年代，我认识了中国香港的张璜先生和美国丁弓良女士，中国台湾的李振兴、陈吉茂和蔡养吾先生，新加坡的林文虎先生，后来又认识了中国上海的马定祥先生和马传德先生。

　　我对雕母的收藏，鲜有人知道。二十年前在《中国钱币》发表过一篇文章，后来公务缠身，匿迹江湖，无暇顾及。现在我将四十年来收藏的近百枚雕母和一些稀有钱币，公诸于世。

　　我的前半生成就，须感谢已去世的皇考，亦要感谢百岁的萱堂。同时我更要感谢我的良伴林慧华，没有她的支持与鼓励，这二十年来的成就是不会实现的。当然我的一对儿女的爱，也给了我精神上的支持。

　　特别鸣谢霍敏仪小姐、蔡雪晶小姐和龙颖思小姐，感谢她们在编辑本书时给予的协助。更感谢杨嵘博士和杨黄慧嬿女士，对本书提供了宝贵的意见，同时感谢郝凤亮先生和李经泰先生为此书的顺利出版而四方奔走。

黄思贤　谨识

二〇一九年十月

PROLOGUE

The first half of my life was bittersweet. I was born in a Chinese village and during my years as an elementary and secondary student, I switched from one school to another because of the surroundings and financial condition, with the consequence that I'm not quite good at Chinese culture or language. Later I went to Hong Kong where I studied for two years in Queen's College and moved to America before long.

I came to California in December 1958 and have settled in Los Angeles from 1959 until now.

I was admitted to University of California, Los Angeles (UCLA) in 1960 and got my bachelor's degree four years later. In the year 1968 I got my doctor's degree from University of South California and have been doing my post-doctoral study since then until 1969. Then I got my degree of Medicine Doctor from UCLA in 1976.

As for research, I have been doing several studies between 1962 and 1984, ranging from optics to laser, from liquid crystals to flat-screen TV, and later I did research on superconductivity (electrical).

I practiced medicine in Los Angeles in 1978, and then was also responsible for management in hospital and healthcare company. With the mission of contributing to the society, I proposed and set up the Sino-America hospital in Shanghai , China, a decade ago.

I was married to Ms. Zheng in 1967, who gave birth to a son and a daughter, but unfortunately she died in 1993.

I was remarried to Ms. Lim and live a happy life together with a successful career. This is the second start of my life.

I have been collecting ancient coins for 40 years. Initially, I bought ordinary coins from antique stores in Chinatowns all over America , bought a dozen of ingots from Mr. E. Kann over 30 years ago and some Kongshoubu (a metallic currency used during the Period of Warring States) and Jincuodao (a metallic currency used under Wang Mang's reign in Han Dynasty) later from Howard Gibbs collection. Then by chance I bought all collections of Mr. Speicher from University of Rochester . This is the start of my collection of ancient coins.

In 1970s and 1980s, I was acquainted with Mr. Zhang Huang from Hong Kong, China and Ms. Ding Gongliang from the States, then with Mr. Li Zhenxing, Mr. Chen Jimao and Mr. Cai Yangwu from Taiwan, China , Mr. Lin Wenhu from Singapore and later with Mr. Ma Dingxiang and Mr. Ma Fude from Shanghai of China.

Recently, few people knew about my collection of Diaomu. I published a paper in China Coin twenty years ago before I was held back by hard work and had to cover my traces. Now I'll bring to light close to a hundred of Diaomu and some rare coins I collected in the past 40 years.

For the achievements in the first half of my life, I owe a lot to my father who has passed away and my mother who is 100 years old. Meanwhile, I am even more grateful for my wife Lin Huihua, without whose support and encouragement, I would not have had my achievements in the recent decade. Certainly the love from my son and daughter gives me spiritual support.

I give my special thanks to Miss Huo Minyi, Miss Cai Xuejing and Miss

Long Yingsi for their assistance in edition of this book. And I'd also like to thank Dr. Yang Rong and Ms Yanghuang Huiyan for their valuable opinions on this book.At the same time, I would like to thank Mr. Hao Fengliang and Mr. Li Jingtai for the smooth publication of this book.

Wong Shin-Yin
OCT.2019

目录
CONTENTS

雕母的讨论

我出生在中国，但年幼便离乡背井，在海外奔波已五十载，集钱的时间亦已有四十多年。这四十多年来，认识的古钱朋友有很多，如中国台湾的蔡养吾、李振兴、陈吉茂，新加坡的林文虎，中国的马定祥先生和马传德先生，美国的丹尼尔·陈。这些朋友，有些事业有成，有些已成故人，真是"雕钱美貌应犹在，只是朱颜改"。

四十多年前在美国收集精美的古钱，是一件难事，想收集一枚雕母，更是难上加难。梦想着，期望着，足足等了十多年。一九八〇年，我的挚友丹尼尔·陈在偶然的机会中收集到两枚雕母（乾隆通宝和道光通宝）和十数枚母钱（包括嘉庆、道光、咸丰各朝母钱）。当时陈先生割爱，相让了两枚道光母钱和一枚咸丰母钱。这是我收集雕母和母钱的开端。我第一次自己收集雕母是十多年前的事，也是一个偶然的机会，美国藏家曾泽禄医师和我都得到了数枚光绪通宝。从此以后，我收藏雕母的成绩，越来越显著。一九八四年，香港古钱拍卖（MONEY CO.），我得到了一枚咸丰当十。一九九〇年，我的挚友丹尼尔·陈不幸病逝，他遗言要将他的古钱藏品全部拍卖，这样，世界各地的古钱泉友可以公平地投拍他的藏品。一九九一年六月，陈先生的全部古钱藏品在美国长堤钱币展览会拍卖，参与竞拍的人士来自世界各地，竞争激烈。荣幸的是陈先生藏品中的两枚雕母，最终归属于我。十年的时间，虽已完成心愿，但每见这两枚雕母，依旧怀念故友，黯然流泪，亦有"十年人事九变更，百年沧海变桑田"之感。

从此，奠定了我集雕母的基础。

最近，中国内地出了很多新的"古泉"书籍，讨论雕母的数据亦有增加，可惜在价格评估方面，比香港和海外拍卖的价格低了许多。例如咸丰雕母当十，国内"古泉"书籍评估大概人民币两三千元，可是十多年前香港拍卖咸丰当十，成交价大概一千多美元（人民币一万元以上）；一九九五年五月，在东京"第六次世界钱币"拍卖会上，咸丰当十的成交价超过三十五万日元（人民币两万元以上）；一九九一年，陈先生藏品的乾隆通宝，成交价超过一千三百美元（人民币一万元以上）。

由此可见，清代雕母在海外的价格昂贵，如果是真品，品相精美的小平雕母，在海外应该值人民币一万元以上，当百、当五百和当千的雕母，其价格应该高于一两万人民币。

当然，收藏是为着兴趣，不应沉迷于它们的价值。收藏和研究古钱，可以了解当时朝代的科技发展水平，因为铸钱要求成本低而产量要高；研究古钱又可以了解各朝各代的政治、经济和文化；再者，古钱每一枚都不尽相同，辨别真伪，难度很高，若能辨别出一枚古钱的假和真，定能有"柳暗花明又一村"之感。

关于雕母文献，以鲍康的《大钱图录》为最早。一九三七年，黄鹏霄的《故宫清钱谱》亦简述雕母铸作过程，现节录部分内容如下。

"许福卿工部景福为宝泉局监督，赠余各钱甚备，并就询局中掌故，辄坩载之。福卿云，每改元铸新钱，先选至洁之象牙刻作钱样，呈钱法堂侍郎鉴定，然后以精铜凿成祖钱，（惟老启盛斋顶带铺精此技，印范不挂沙）其穿孔（局呼金口）非钱局人不能凿，再用祖钱翻砂铸母钱，以后开铸，则悉用母钱印范，颁发各省者，亦谓之母钱，外省呈进者为样钱。咸丰朝各省初铸当十钱，率以二成与制钱搭配试行。初尚相安，未几即仍重制钱，当十者，一枚仅当二三文，因而渐废当百当五百当仟者，所铸尤少，惟都中市肆，流布尚多，诸品既废之后，则相率持当百以上诸钱赴质库取物，质库弗敢拒也。案每遇建元，局中例精铸制钱万，当十钱千呈进，谓之万选钱。

"案同治初元，各省亦颁有当十母钱，但未经鼓铸或仅呈样钱塞责，故少流传录中未载。

"乾隆二十四年（1759年）平定回疆，'回疆底定，复有红钱，加铸回文，并令后世子孙永奉其年号，以炫武功'。"

《故宫清钱谱》：

"殿之祖钱，母钱，样钱，凡铸钱之法，先将净铜錾凿成二钱三分者约祖钱，随铸造一钱六七分不等约母钱，然后即铸制钱，每遇更定钱制，例先将钱式进呈，其直省开局之始，亦例由户局先铸祖钱、母钱及制钱各一文，颁发各省，令照式鼓铸（见通考）。端凝殿之京局呈进钱，钱局岁十二月例精铸制钱若干缮呈进，谓之桂镫钱（见户部则例及鲍康大钱图录）。又称大制钱（见内务府广储司则例）。永铸宫与内务府之库储钱，均属菁华所聚，典制攸关，文献幸存，考证有赖。爰依朝代之先后，汰其重复，得二百八十四品汇影成谱，聊供研究币制学者之一著。民国二十六年（1937年）黄鹏霄序。"

一、母钱翻砂铸钱 （表二）

张志中认为：随着铸钱技术的改进，自隋唐至清末，改用母钱铸钱法。铸钱的要求已很严格，每逢改元铸新钱，先作样钱呈帝王审定，《谭宾录》就有记载："武德初行开元通宝钱，初进样目……"隋唐因战乱，历史资料已不可考，只能从清代铸新钱的程序加以推测。清代每铸新钱，户、工二局的程序是：象牙样钱（以上好象牙精雕细刻而成）→铜雕祖钱→初铸母钱→印范母钱→进呈样钱。外省钱局的程序是：初铸母钱（部颁样钱）→印范母钱→进呈样钱。照钱样做祖钱，用祖钱印范铸母钱，再用母钱翻砂铸样钱（进呈样钱），进呈批准后即可大量铸钱，投入市面流通。此时铸钱量虽很大，但都出自数量有限的祖钱，所以规整精，同版钱很多，钱体面，背直观无砂眼。一个由国家控制的铸钱局，均由经验丰富的铸工组成，且铸工大多一生只操此业，在监工督导下决不许次品（有砂眼者）流入市面。

二、铜铸祖钱和初铸母钱

《古钱的鉴定和保养》一书中说："母钱，实际上就是钱模，按照加工方法的不同，可分为雕母和铸母两种。"

雕母有木、牙、锡和铜四种质地。木、牙雕母主要是作为样钱，供呈皇帝选审之用。铜、锡雕母主要用于翻铸雕母，称为"祖钱"。锡雕母则多用于直接铸钱，《天工开物》明确记载有："以母钱百文，用锡雕成。"

张志中说："祖钱雕制精良，文字端庄大方，铜制呈金黄色，地章平整（也有地章微鼓者），穿孔呈方形，轮脊低平。从以上情况分析，作为一枚雕母，首先应具备金黄色的铜质，铜材的颜色分多种，所谓金黄色铜质是经过九炼的铜材，清代的风磨铜由高丽进贡，康熙通宝罗汉钱与流通中的制钱相比，已很细致，若与雕母铜质相比，只能达到四炼而已。

"铜雕母的钱文精美，字口深峻，笔划比同版的流通钱略瘦挺拔，钱缘轮廓与字口同样深峻，内廓和钱穿亦颇规整。雕母钱通体精细，俗称'刀痕化尽'，雕刻痕迹虽已被修饰掉了，若仔细观察，仍能寻到镂刻的痕迹。鉴定雕母时注意钱体应为金黄色，较流通钱稍大一些，厚重，文字略瘦挺拔，地章应有镂雕痕迹。

"母钱，是以祖钱翻砂铸成的钱，为了以后大批开铸，即以此钱制成多枚印范母钱。外省开铸所用母钱，均由工部、户部颁发，称部颁母钱。母钱的特征：钱径小于祖钱（雕母），但略大于一般流通钱。铜制较好，钱的外缘轮、内廓穿口和字口深峻不及雕母，钱文笔划仍纤细挺拔，但逊于雕母。钱体上已不见雕痕，个别母钱如细看仍可发现雕痕。"

《古钱的保养和鉴定》一书中说："较难辨识的是一些清代'雕母'伪品。由于清代距今不远，而雕母大多无锈，伪造者可省去做假锈这一过程。传闻民国初年尚有少数原清代钱局之雕模工人，因出于生计，曾仿制过一些雕母，但这种仿制品与真品毕竟有所不同。凡真品雕母，都用精铜雕成，色泽金黄，雕工认真，能做到刀痕尽化，和镜面一样光润，文字也生动自然。伪品在这几方面往往有所不及。有些咸丰雕母，文字四周底凸起，不及道光之前的平整光洁，雍正以及明代雕母，雕刻工艺水平更高，也更罕见。

"还有一种雕母伪品是选择精美的母钱加工而成。因为母钱是翻砂而成，铜质较粗，与精铜雕成的真品不同，且铸成的穿孔也与手工雕凿的有区别。"

三、刻铸时间

在目前存世文献的讨论中，就雕母方面，只提及清朝期间的雕母是真，民国雇工匠所雕的雕母是伪。

现在看来，光绪、宣统的小平雕母，可以确定地说是光绪年间或是宣统年间雕刻的。咸丰大钱和一部分小平可以说是咸丰年雕刻。但是顺治、雍正、乾隆、嘉庆或道光的雕母，就很难确定其是当代雕刻品还是后世的雕刻品。如一九九二年泰星在香港拍卖，有一枚宝川当百，马定祥先生说是后世雕刻品，但原因何在，马先生并没有真正说明。最近《宝苏局钱币》一书中，有记载由乾隆到同治时的宝苏局雕母钱，认为"至今发现的宝苏局雕母钱，乾隆以后各种纪年基本齐全。若以此与相应都颁各省之样钱，或户部自用之雕母钱进行比较，它们在风格上存在较大的区别，可知这些雕母确是宝苏局自行镌刻的。""可见各省钱局自行镌刻雕母钱，虽然在钱市之铸造上，存在很大的方便，但给地方钱局的营利弊，亦大开了绿灯。"可还有疑问是，这些宝苏局雕母钱，亦可以是清代私人铸刻的或后世铸刻的。这些问题，还要请古泉学者多做一番工作来解释，希望不久的将来能得到答案。

表一把上面的问题简单地列出，以便读者参考和研究。

鉴定一枚钱是不是雕母不难，但确定其是当代所雕还是后世所雕则不是一件易事。正如嘉庆通宝雕母，笔者藏有三四枚，它们都是金黄色，厚重，金口未开，雕工精美绝伦，铁划银钩，鬼斧神工，刀痕尽化。可惜到现在为止，还没有办法确定它们是嘉庆当代所雕还是后世所雕。

表一 刻铸时间表

	中央官雕	省、地方官雕或私雕
清朝	同期（当代）	同期（当代）
	后世	后世（？）
民国	伪雕	伪雕

四、铜质金色的疑问

中央所雕刻的雕母大多呈金黄色，大概是用了精美的黄铜之故。有人说："红铜七成，锌三成可炼成黄铜，经二次回炉精炼可作样钱铜材，经四次精炼（回炉）可作雕母铜材。"

鲍康《大钱图录》说："以精铜凿成祖钱……为老启盛斋顶带铺精……。"由此可见，雕母不一定由工部或户部工匠铸，所以真正雕母之合金，不一定一致，成色不同，雕母不一定完全是金黄色的。

再者，由雍正至宣统，历时一百多年，所以雕母铜质不可能是千篇一律的。又有些未开金口而又用来铸过母钱的雕母，其表面铜质又发生化学变化，所以到现在也许不可能再呈金黄色了。

有人说，工部进呈的雕母，一定是铜质精美，呈金黄色。但用来铸母钱的，不一定用成色好的精铜，而且雕工亦不用十全十美。

这里可以大胆地推论，真正的雕母不一定是金黄色的，雕工不一定是刀痕尽化，亦不一定是平滑如镜的。

五、雕母和初铸母钱的区别（图1、图2、图3、图4）

近年来，讨论祖钱（雕母）和母钱的文献颇多，形成了一个集钱的新风潮。可惜，有很多文献东抄西集，拓本不好，图片和照片亦不清楚，有时会给人鱼目混珠之感。仔细看图片中所谓的雕母，实为母钱。雕母是雕的，每一划都是铁划银钩，钱没有砂眼或流铜，雕母无论怎样完善都可能找到刀痕或凿痕，这些刀痕或凿痕，用十倍的放大镜看，每一刀每一痕都是清简玲珑。有时刀痕太大，铸出来的母钱亦会有刀痕，但这些铸的刀痕，是不尖锐的。集泉家要小心注意，不然的话，把母钱当成雕母，就失去了集泉的意义了。

再者，如果雕母地章是突起的话，初铸母钱地章也一定是突起的，且初铸母钱比原本雕母直径细一些，而未开穿的雕母，横切面边沿儿和内廓是成直角的；开金口的雕母，边沿儿比较圆，内廓呈三角状，而初铸母钱，沿儿亦是成三角状的。

六、初铸母钱和程序（表二）

清代铸钱，是用母钱做成钱树，然后翻砂铸钱，现在流传下来的钱树实物为数颇多。但由雕母翻砂铸钱，程序如何，文字记载不详，这些母钱可能不是用雕母做成钱树后铸造出来的。那么怎么用雕母铸母钱呢？现在很难说，但从铸母实物验查，砂眼很少地章平滑，如果用平常的翻砂铸钱方法是不可能的。如果真是用翻砂法，用的沙一定比普通铸钱的沙更幼细，而且铸母钱的程序一定不同。可不可能用失蜡法由雕母铸造母钱呢？到现在还是一个谜。

铸成初铸母钱，修改和加工程序又如何呢？现在亦是一个谜。真正初铸的母钱，笔划虽然比雕母粗一些，但仅用肉眼观察，很多时候是分不出来的。

初铸母钱，字口深峻，有时还能隐约辨别出刀工痕迹。一般在钱的边缘上，保留拔模斜度，而和"雕母"的共同之处，都是钱体较一般钱稍大，制作精良，币材铜质光泽，钱体较厚重。

和普通钱比较起来，母钱笔划比同版的流通钱略瘦、挺拔，钱缘轮廓与字口同样深峻，内部和钱穿亦颇规整。

表二　清代铸新钱的程序

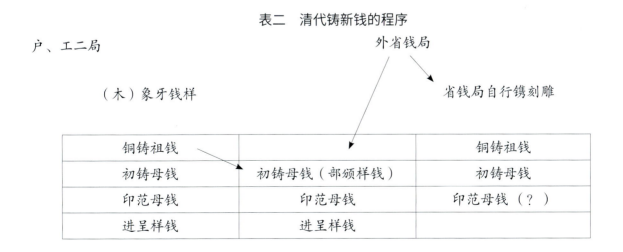

户、工二局		外省钱局	
（木）象牙钱样			省钱局自行镌刻雕
铜铸祖钱			铜铸祖钱
初铸母钱	初铸母钱（部颁样钱）		初铸母钱
印范母钱	印范母钱		印范母钱（？）
进呈样钱	进呈样钱		

雕母是雕刻出来的，如果用十倍放大镜观察，差不多每一枚雕母都会呈现雕痕。雕母的刀痕是锋利的，像刀切过一样，痕的线条明显，如果这些线条是粗而深的话，雕出来的初铸母钱亦会有这样的线条，可惜母钱的线条是粗的，而且线条边又有凹凸不平之感，请泉友留心。

七、母钱与样钱

孙仲汇说："凡正式铸钱的雕母中间的方孔已经开好，一般微呈四决，钱局内称方孔为金口，开金口需要很高的技术，否则铸造时容易黏沙。"

"……按旧例钱局中新铸钱成，需呈送有关当局核审，称进呈样钱，而中央户、工二部为统一国内钱式，也精铸一批铜钱颁发各路，分部颁母钱和部颁样钱两种。样钱比普通钱精美，钱形稍大，钱肉平整，文字峻削，轮廓穿内都仔细锉磨，方圆特别标准。母钱的形制和样钱稍异，因防止印范时黏沙，故轮廓微成圆口，周边突起如鱼脊，钱文笔划较样钱细瘦，细微处亦点划分明，肉质更为光洁。"

八、雕母常见的刀痕（图5、图6）

既然雕母是雕刻出来的，当然有雕刻的工具，这些工具是什么？现在已很难知道，各朝有没有改变呢？这问题亦很难回答。据推论，刻雕母用的主要工具应该有：圆规、刀、锉、锯、钻等，以前面四种工具的留痕最为显著且有实物为证。

如果仔细看雕母内外廓的钱面，有少部分的雕母还留有圆规的痕迹，通常是在外廓的内部或内廓的外部。

在地章，通常靠近外廓边沿儿会留下很深的刀痕，这种情形亦可以在接近四方内廓边沿儿处找到。而在地章亦常常找到刀痕或三角形的凿痕。

在直划的边沿儿，亦可以找到直的刀痕或横的刀痕。这些刀痕都是有规律的，而且大多数是肉眼看不到的。

有些半圆形的划，如满文的"宝"字，字划半圆形肉缘，有参差不齐的直划或横划。有些字划成四方形的口状或长方形状。这方形或长方形线条内部深下去成"X"形或两个倒"Y"形，它们是很有规则的，未知民国的雕母有没有这样严格呢？

又有圆形的文字内部成圆尖形。

所以结论是：好的雕母，当雕工雕刻它们的时候，字划雕技是有一定规则的。

九、雕母雕技的演变 （图7）

雕母雕技的演变有些地方亦是很明显的，正如乾隆雕母地章大多平坦。道光开始，以后各朝小平雕母很少地章平坦，大部分是凸起的。

雕母字划的演变最是明显，乾隆雕母，雕工绝伦，边沿通常不斜，和地章成差不多九十度角，而且字划宽阔；嘉庆以后，字划变为瘦而狭；到光绪时期，大部分字划幼细如丝，字划边沿儿与地章再不成直角，而是变为斜角，甚至到四十五度。这种改变是否美观暂且不说，但对于翻砂铸钱仅技术的进步上，有何意义，只待以后研究了。

十、满文"宝"字的演变（图8）

满文"宝"字的演变值得讨论，尤其"宝"字对内廓的垂横意义重大，乾隆嘉庆时期的雕母，"宝"字垂横划成（⌐）状，是起角的。到道光时期，这垂横划又呈弘形状（⌒），没有起角之感，到咸丰光绪之时，又呈圆形之感（⌒），这或是雕刻技艺的改变，现在已无从考证了。但如果乾隆嘉庆的雕母，宝字垂横是（⌐）状，而又起角的，那么这些雕母是当代雕刻的可能性是极高的，希望以后能收藏到更多真正的乾隆当代雕母，用以解答这个问题。

十一、雕母各种做形技术

各种雕母并不是同时雕刻，也不是同一工匠雕刻，铜质亦不一定一致，有时有些雕母是鎏金的，色泽当然会有些改变，所以每一枚雕母都有它自身的特征。

总的来说，雕母做形，多彩多姿，美不胜收。曾见乾隆雕母，雕工绝伦，笔划清晰深峻，直而没有斜度，地章平坦，平滑如镜。细观察，刀横是直落，所以字划有凹凸不平之感，但整个钱雕工秀丽而绝伦，只是雕于何时，是真是假，还要多些研究。

光绪通宝小平，传世亦不少，可惜雕工多半拙劣，地章凸起，刀痕亦多，笔划尖瘦如丝，划边极斜，如三角锉，满文宝字留痕甚多，刀痕和字划成正角。光绪雕母拓本，字划细如毛发，很精美，可惜实物用放大镜细审，雕工粗老，毫无美感可言。有些光绪雕母，雕工不精，或像未成品，此类雕刻，地章凸起，而地章光滑中还带刀痕，钱的字划亦比较崎岖参差。但其中，有小部分，雕工亦很精美。

咸丰大钱，尤其是宝源宝泉当百当千大钱，雕工精美绝伦，可以和乾隆当代雕刻钱媲美。这些大钱，地章真是平滑如镜，刀痕尽化，笔划又有铁划银钩之感，让人爱不释手。

咸丰小平，大部分雕工精美，一般来说，它笔划窄过乾隆雕母，但是宽过光绪雕母，笔划偏斜，但没有光绪雕母那样极端。背面满文宝字，刀痕是顺文的，与光绪雕母的刀痕和字划成正角不同。咸丰小平雕母，大部分地章是凸起的。

宣统雕母，笔者认为假的比真的多。宣统通宝雕母，目前只有小平（宝泉）大样和小样，雕工和光绪雕母差不多。但伪雕的亦很多，通常拓本看不出，伪雕的实物用放大镜细看，刻的笔划，不伦不类，凹凸不清，到处都是刀痕，一点儿神都没有，一点儿美感都没有，泉家一定要小心。

有一种嘉庆通宝，"嘉"字最大横划，正直倒像机器制造的，但用十倍放大镜细看，这些长直的横划是雕的。

现在，收藏和研究雕母更为专业，咸丰光绪时期雕母的真假，因为实物比较多，鉴定比较容易。乾隆时期的雕母实物亦多，后世雕刻的亦多，容易鱼目混珠。至于雍正、嘉庆、道光各朝，更难分别。

《丁福保钱谱》记载的雕母亦寥寥可数，而黄鹏霄的《故宫清钱谱》书中记载雕母尤以嘉庆、道光、咸丰各朝最多，可惜现在没有实物考证，所记各钱是摹本又不是拓本，真假难分，实在可惜。

现时期的文献中，记载雕母的很多，可惜多是拓本，是雕母还是母钱，很难确定；部分文献有照片，可惜照片模糊不清，不能辨别雕母的庐山真面目。

　　我们已踏入了一个新纪元，研究古钱亦不能马虎，要实事求是，给出正确的理论依据。当然，研究不一定正确，推广不一定得当，但总比没有根据的推测有意义。

　　以上举例，寥寥数种，望海内外泉友将来能在这方面下功夫，使埋没于世的泉中之王——雕母呈现于世人眼前。

　　笔者认为中国古泉学会应组织相关专家对雕母古钱进行研究。这样既对研究古钱意义重大，又可以让后代泉家有所借鉴。

图1　祖钱（雕母）

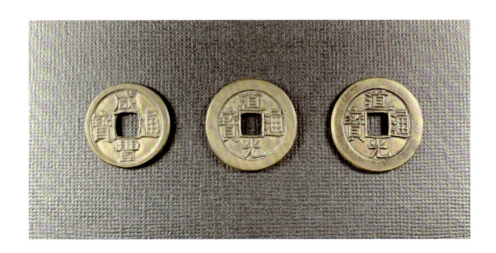

图 2　母钱

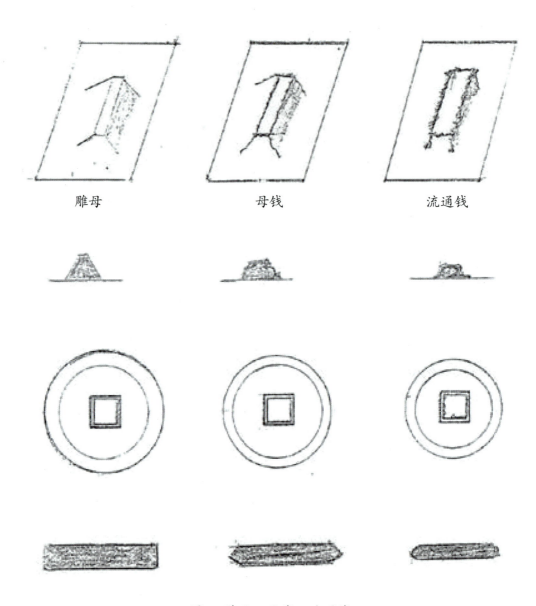

雕母　　　　　　　　母钱　　　　　　　　流通钱

图3　雕母·母钱·流通钱

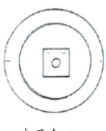
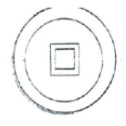
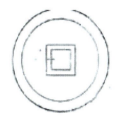

未开金口　　　　　　　　　　初铸母钱　　　　　　　　　　开金口

图4　外廓的演变

雕母

母钱

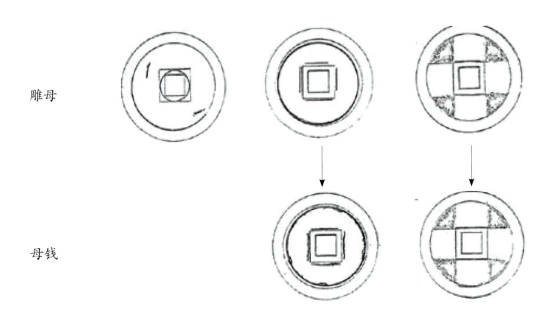

图5　刀痕或凿痕

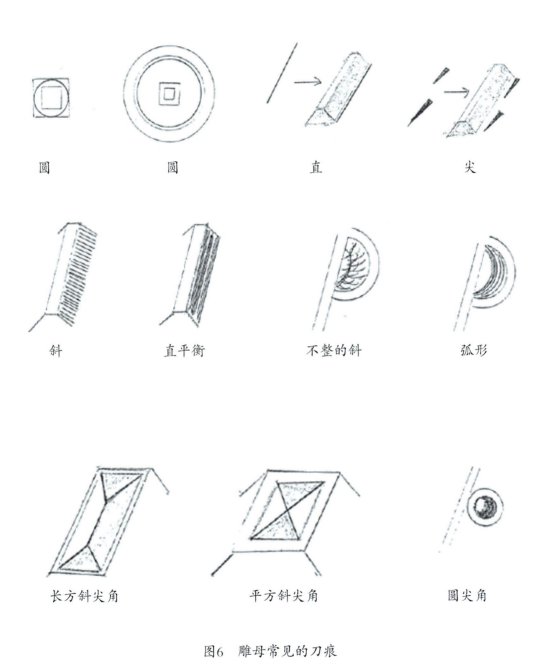

圆　　　　　　圆　　　　　　直　　　　　　尖

斜　　　　　直平衡　　　　不整的斜　　　　弧形

长方斜尖角　　　　　平方斜尖角　　　　　圆尖角

图6　雕母常见的刀痕

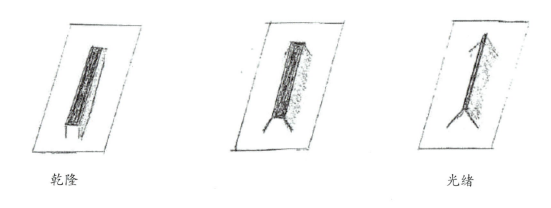

乾隆　　　　　　　　　　　　　　　　　光绪

图7　雕母雕技的演变

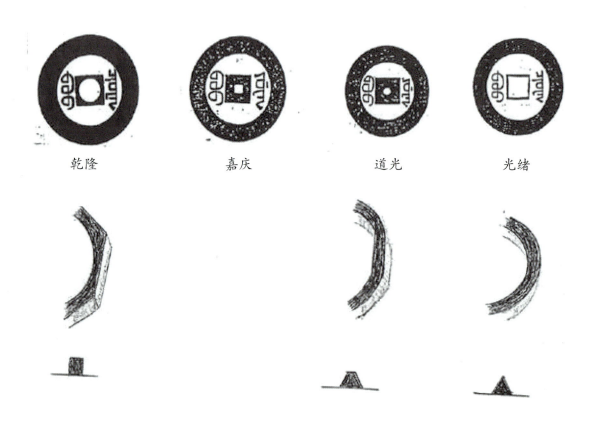

乾隆　　　　　嘉庆　　　　　道光　　　　　光绪

图8　满文汉字的演变

DISCUSSION ON DIAOMU

Although born in China, I left home in childhood and have been living overseas for fifty years. I have been collecting money for more than thirty years and got to know many friends with the same interests, like Cai Yangwu, Li Zhenxing, Chen Jimao in Taiwan, China, LinWenhu in Singapore, Ma Dingxiang and Ma Fude in the mainland of China and Daniel Chen in the US. Among those friends, some were very successful in their career, unfortunately some has passed away. It is truly that "Beautiful Diaomu is still there, but the people are not".

During these forty years, collecting delicate ancient money has been difficult still, it was even more to collect Diaomu. I have been waiting for more than a decade in my dreams and wishes. About the year 1980, my close friend, Daniel Chen collected two Diaomu (QianLong Tongbao and DaoGuang Tongbao) and a dozen of mother money (that in JiaJing, DaoGuang and XianFeng periods) by coincidence. Mr. Chen gave up what he treasured at that time and transferred to me two DaoGuang mother coins and a XianFeng mother coin. This is the beginning of my collection of Diaomu and mother money. It was ten years ago that I collected the first Diaomu. On a rare occasion, Doc. Zeng Zelu, an American collector, and I both got several GuangXu Tongbao. Ever since then, I achieved more and more in collecting Diaomu. At an auction of ancient money (Money Co.) in Hong Kong in 1984, I got a XianFeng equivalent to ten. In 1990, my close friend Daniel Chen passed away and he said in his will to auction all of his collections of ancient money, such that quan pals all over the world could bid for his collections in fairness. On June 1991, all of Mr. Chen's collections were shown in Long Beach Coin Show in the US, people came from every corners of the world and there was a quite competition. I was happy to get his two Diaomu finally. My wishes ten years ago came true. Despite this, I am very sad thinking of my old friend whenever I cast sight on the two Diaomu. Isn't it "too much has changed in a decade and the seas have turned into farmland"? （Rubbing 1, and fig. 1 and 2）

This lays the foundation for my collection of Diaomu.

Recently, several new books on ancient quan have been published in the mainland of China, and materials on Diaomu has increased slightly, but pricewise, it is several fold cheaper than that Hong Kong, China and overseas. Take a XianFeng Diaomu equivalent to ten for example, it is evaluated at about 2 to 3 thousand RMB by domestic ancient quan books, however, about a decade ago in an auction in Hong Kong, hammer price of the money was more than a thousand US dollars （more than ten thousand RMB）, and in Tokyo in May 1995 at the Sixth International Money Auction, hammer price of （item 1234） XianFeng equivalent to ten was over 350,000 yin （more than twenty thousand RMB）, and in 1991, the hammer price of QianLong Tongbao in Chen's collection was over 1,300 US dollars （more than ten thousand RMB）

It can be seen that Diaomu of Qing Dynasty costs a lot overseas. If it was a small genuine, delicate ping Diaomu, it is worth more than ten thousand RMB in a foreign land. For Diaomu equivalent to a hundred, five hundred or a thousand, the price should be higher than ten to twenty thousand RMB.

Certainly, we collect ancient money for interest, and should not care too much for their value. Collection and study of ancient quan helps to find out technology in a certain dynasty, because the production is supposed to be high at a low cost in making money. Studying ancient money also helps to learn about politics and economy in each dynasty. Compared with collecting stamps, collecting ancient money is more meaningful. In addition, ancient money is different from each other, it is sometimes very difficult to tell the fake from the genuine, so when we are able to differentiate, we sure would feel "there is always light at the end of the tunnel".

Daqian Tulu by Bao Kang is the earliest among literatures to talk about Diaomu, and *Recording of Qing Money in the Palace Museum* by Huang Pengxiao in 1937 also described briefly the process of making Diaomu. The following is from the two books.

"Xu Fuqing, jingfu from Ministry of Works, supervisor of BaoQuan bureau, gave me one of each kind of money and told me the detail about making money, and I recorded as the following. Fuqing said that, each time a reform was made to cast new money, ivory of extremely clean was selected to make sample money and submitted to the assistant minister of Money Administration for review, then ancestor money was made of refined copper, (only was an expert on this and left on sand on the printed mold), the hole (called opening of the gold mouth) could only be done by workers of the bureau, then mother money was made after ancestor money by sand-casting, and then money started to be made, that was, printed mold of mother money was distributed to each province and what was submitted by another province was called sample money. Each province in XianFeng's period casted money equivalent to ten at the first place, and one fifth of the money accompanied pattern money in a trial. Initially the reform was settled, but as time went on, new money had to be made. Money equivalent to ten previously might only be equivalent to two or three wen, and the decrease happened to money equivalent to a hundred, five hundred and a thousand. Only that, in the market a lot was distributed, afterwards, more than too often money equivalent to over a hundred was taken to withdraw goods from pawnshops, which dared not to refuse. As a rule, whenever new money was to be made, the bureau would cast ten thousand of refined coins and submitted as ten coins of a thousand which was called Wanxuan money (a coin that is one in a million) [Tulu]

"In early years of TongZhi period, mother coins equivalent to ten were issued in each province, but they were not minted by melting metals or were only submitted as sample coins, so few of them were not handed down and they were not recorded in literatures [Tulu]

"In the 24th year of QianLong period, 'Huijiang was pacified and after the pacification, there were red coins again with hui language in them and the later generation were ordered to adopt his reign title to show off his military success'."

Recording of Qing Money in the Palace Museum:

Finally ancestor, mother and sample money, "In all methods for making money, pure copper was made into ancestor money of two qian and three fen, then mother money of one qian and six or seven fen, then money. Whenever the money-making mechanism was modified, the money patterns were submitted in the first place, starting from the directly supervising bureau. As a rule, the bureau made each one of ancestor coin, mother coin and pattern coin and distributed them for each province to make money after." (See Tongkao). Capital bureau in Duanning palace submitted coin, "as a rule, in December the bureau made several coins and submitted it, called Guideng money". (See regulations by Ministry of Revenue and *Daqian Tulu* by Bao Kang) It was also called large pattern money (see regulations by the Department of Supplies in Ministry of Internal Order). Stock money in Yongshou Palace and Ministry of Internal Order was made of the best material. This is relevant with regulations so that we can still see the recordings for evidenced research.

Depending on time order of dynasties, deleting the replicates, 284 coins were photocopied and made into a book for scholars studying money. 26th year of the Republic of China, prologue by Huang Pengxiao.

1. Making money after mother coins by sand-casting (table 2)

Zhang Zhizhong said: With improvement in money-making techniques, money was made after mother coins from Sui and Tang Dynasties to the end of Qing Dynasty. The requirements were rather strict by then, that was, in the case of reform to make new money, the samples were submitted to the emperor for review and it was recorded in *Tan Bao lu* that: "when Kaiyuan Tongbao was first issued in Wude period, the samples initially submitted…". Historical records of Sui and Tang Dynasties were unavailable due to wars and can only be speculated from procedures of making new money in Qing Dynasties. Whenever new money was made in Qing Dynasties, procedures in the bureau under Ministry of Revenue and Ministry of Works were: ivory sample money (carefully carved from good-quality ivory) → copper ancestor money → initially carved mother money → printed mold mother money → submitted sample money. The procedures in each province were: initially carved mother money (sample money issued by the departments) → printed mold mother money → submitted sample money. Ancestor money was made after sample money, printed mold mother money was made after ancestor money, sample money (submitted sample money) after mother money by sand-casting, and money could be casted in batches after approval and circulate in the market. Although the amount of coins made was huge, they were all casted after ancestor money, so they were neat, many of them were of the same batch, plus they looked nice and there were no sand holes when examined grossly. A bureau controlled by the central government boasted workers with rich experiences, and most of them did the job for life. Defective products (those with sand holes) were not allowed to circulate in the market under rigorous supervision.

2. Copper ancestor money and initially casted mother money

It was said in *Authentication and Maintenance of Ancient Coins* that, "Mother money, money pattern, actually, can be classified into Diaomu and Zhumu according to their processing methods".

Diaomu were of four types in terms of nature, wood, ivory, tin and copper. Diaomu of wood and teeth were mainly used as sample money to be submitted to the emperor for selection. Diaomu of copper and tin were mainly used for Zhumu to be made after and were called "ancestor money". Tin Diaomu was mostly used for money to be casted directly after as was explicitly written in Tiangongkaiwu that "A hundred of mother coins were made of tin".

It was also said by Zhang Zhizhong that, "Ancestor coins were carved with great care, so that the copper looked golden, bottom seal was flat (some bottom seal was protruding slightly), the hollow in the middle was square and the ring back was low and flat. Seen from the above, as a Diaomu, first, its copper should look golden. Copper materials were of several colors and the golden one was made after refining of nine times. Windmill copper in Qing Dynasty was given as tribute by Korea. Kangxi Tongbao arhat money was more refined in terms of the copper material than pattern money in circulation, but compared to copper Diaomu, it just reached the level of refining of four times".

Characters of copper Diaomu were exquisite, cuts of the words were deep, the strokes looked thinner and straighter than those of coins of the same edition in circulation, outline of the rim was deep as the cut of words, the inner outline and the Chuan were in order as well. Diaomu was delicate in all aspects, which was commonly called "elimination of knife marks". Although traces of carving were invisible after embellishment, if a XiZhou was observed carefully, they could still be found. In authentication of Diaomu, it should be borne in mind that the body should be golden, a little bigger than coins in circulation, thick and heavy, the characters are thin and straight, and there should be no traces of carving on the bottom seal.

Mother coins, casted after ancestor money by sand-casting, were used for several printed mold mother coins to be casted after for later money-making in batches. Characters of mother money: its diameter was less than that of ancestor money (Diaomu), yet more than common money in circulation; the copper was quite good; the ring outline of its outer rim, Chuan cuts of the inner outline and cuts of words were not as deep as those of Diaomu; strokes of the characters remained thin and straight, but not comparable to those of Diaomu; knife marks were not visible in the body, but there were traces of carving in some mother coins, just like XiZhou.

The book about *Authentication and Maintenance of Ancient Money* was also read that, "Some counterfeit Qing Diaomu were difficult to be told apart. Since Qing Dynasty is not far away from today, most Diaomu of this period have no rust, and the counterfeiters do not have to make fake rust. It was said that in the early years of the Republic of China, some former carvers working in money bureau of Qing Dynasty had made some Diaomu to make a living. However, these Diaomu were somewhat different from the genuine ones after all. Each genuine Diaomu, made of refined copper, was golden in color, exquisite in craftsmanship capable of making the knife marks disappear, smooth like a mirror and has vivid and natural characters. The fake ones are inferior in these aspects. For some XianFeng Diaomu, the surrounding of characters is protruding, not as smooth and clean as those before DaoGuang period. Diaomu of yongzheng period or Ming Dynasty have even better craftsmanship and are even more rare.

"There is another kind of fake Diaomu prepared from refined mother coins. Since mother coins were made by sand-casting and the copper it was made of was rather coarse, the Diaomu resulted were different from the genuine ones made of refined copper, and the holes were different from those chiseled manually."

3. Carving time

Discussion on Diaomu in literatures up to now also suggested that Diaomu in Qing Dynasty were genuine, while those made by workers in years of the Republic of China were fake.

Today, we can say with confidence that the small ping Diaomu in GuangXu and XuanTong's periods were made in the periods respectively. However, it is difficult to determine whether Diaomu in ShunZhi, yongzheng, QianLong, JiaQing or DaoGuang's period were made in their period respectively or in later ages. For instance, Taixing made an auction in Hong Kong in 1992 for a baoChuan equivalent to a hundred, which, according to Ma Dingxiang, was carved in later ages. But he did not say exactly why. Recently, in the book *Baosu Bureau Money* (Shanghai Classics Publishing House) , Baosu Diaomu from QianLong to Tongzhi's period were recorded. The authors believed that for Baosu bureau Diaomu discovered up to now, those in ages after QianLong's period are basically complete. If compared with sample coins distributed to each province or Diaomu used inside the Ministry of Revenue, these Diaomu are quite different in terms of style and it can be seen that these Diaomu were definitely made by Baosu bureau. They also said that, "we can see that money bureau of each province made Diaomu on its own, although this is of great convenience to money-making, but it also encouraged fraudulent practices in local money bureaus." A further problem is that these Baosu Diaomu could also be made in private in Qing Dynasty or by later generations. More work by scholars of ancient quan is necessary to explain these questions. I hope we can get the answers in the near future.

Table 1 gives a list of the questions above for the readers' reference and research.

Authentication of Diaomu is not difficult, but that of a genuine Diaomu made in the contemporary period is not. Take JiaQing Tongbao Diaomu for example. I have three or four of them, all of which are golden, thick and heavy, with gold mouth closal. They were carved beautifully with sturdy strokes and lines, excellent craftsmanship and almost without knife marks. Unfortunately, it still can not be determined whether they were carved in the contemporary JiaQing period or in later ages.

4.Question on copper being golden

Diaomu made under the central government was golden, probably because refined brass was used. It was said that red copper of 70% plus zinc of 30% could produce brass after two times of refinement and could be used as copper for Diaomu after four times of refinement.

Bao Kang said in his *DaqianTulu* that ... ancestor money was made of refined copper... only... It can be seen that Diaomu was not necessarily made by works in the Ministry of Works or the Ministry of Revenue, so alloy of genuine Diaomu might inconsistent in nature or color, and Diaomu was not necessarily golden.

Besides, during more than a hundred years from YongZheng to XuanTong's period, copper for Diaomu was impossibly to be exactly the same. What's more, some Diaomu with their golden mouth closed was gilded, and the color was brightly golden. Whether they were Diaomu for submission is unknown.

It was also said that Diaomu submitted by the Ministry of Works must have been golden ones made of refined copper, but those used for casting mother money were not necessarily made of refined copper, and the craftsmanship was not necessarily perfect either.

A bold deduction can be made here that not all of the genuine Diaomu were necessarily golden, and the craftsmanship was not necessarily so good that no knife marks were visible, or surfaces of the Diaomu were smooth as a mirror.

5.Differences between Diaomu and mother money initially made（Figure 1,2,3,4）

There has been a great deal of literatures talking about ancestor money（Diaomu）, which, we can say, is a new epoch for money collection. Unfortunately, quite a few literatures patched relevant information together.As a result, the rubbing is not good, so are pictures and photos, causing people to pass fish eyes for pearls. Observed carefully, the so-called Diaomu in such literatures was actually mother money. Diaomu was carved and each stroke was strong and sturdy. Coins got no sand holes or copper flowing, but Diaomu had knife marks or chisel marks no matter how perfect they were. Under an amplifier 10 power, each blade and trace can be seen clearly. Sometimes, a trace of blade was too big and the money coins made after would have a trace as well. However, the knife marks were not sharp. Collectors should be careful, otherwise, basic principles for collecting quan would be lost if mother coins were taken for Diaomu.

In addition, if the bottom seal of Diaomu was protruding, that of mother coins made after would certainly be so. The diameter of mother coins initially made was thinner than that of Diaomu. To Diaomu without a hole in the middle, there was a right angle between the rims of crossing section and the inner outline, while to those with its gold mouth opened, the rims were rather round and the angle is a triangle. To mother coins initially made, the rims constituted a triangle.

6.mother money Initially made and procedures（table 2）

In money-making of Qing Dynasty, mother coins formed a tree to make coins after by sand-casting, so there are many money trees existent today. However, there is little information in literatures on the procedures of making coins after Diaomu by sand-casting. One can say that it is unlikely to have Diaomu form a tree and make mother coins. How were mother coins made after Diaomu？ This is difficult to say, but based on examination on actual ZhuMu, which had few sand holes and smooth bottom stamp, It is impossible to make coins by sand-casting as usual. If coins were truly made by sand-casting, the sand used must have been finer than used in common money-making process and the procedures to make mother coins must have been different. Is it possible that mother coins were made after Diaomu by wax-losing？ This is still unknown.

What were the procedures for modifying and refining mother coins initially made？ This is unknown too. Although seen with naked eyes, strokes of genuine mother coins initially made were bolder than those of Diaomu, they could not be differentiated in most cases.

Cuts of characters of mother coins initially made were very deep. Knife marks could be seen sometimes. Usually, slope of removing the mold was reserved on rims of coins, and the common with Diaomu was larger coins than common ones, great craftsmanship, glowing copper material and heavy coin body.

Compared with common coins, strokes of mother coins were thinner and straighter than coins in circulation of the same edition. Besides, outline of the rims of coins was as deep as cuts of characters, and the inside and the Chuan were quite neat too.

Diaomu was carved and the traces could be seen under an amplifier 10 power in almost every Diaomu. Just like what was said before, the carving traces of Diaomu were sharp, as if they were cut with a knife. The traces had clear-cut lines, and if these lines were bold and deep, mother coins initially made made after had these lines too. It was a pity that the lines of Diaomu were bold, and rims of the lines were uneven as well. Quan pals please pay attention.

7.Mother money and sample money

It was said by Sun Zhonghui that, "the square hole in the middle of Diaomu officially used to make money was opened already, and it was usually protruding in four directions. The square hole was called golden mouth by professionals in money-making bureau It took exquisite techniques to open it, otherwise, sand would stick into the coins resulted."

"... As a rule, whenever new coins were made in the bureau, they had to be submitted to relevant authority for review, therefore they were called sample coins for submission. Besides, in order to unify money pattern nationwide, Ministry of Revenue and Ministry of Works in the central government also made a batch of refi ned copper coins to be distributed and these coins were categorized into two types, mother coins issued by the Ministry and sample coins by the Ministry. Sample coins were more delicate than common ones, with slightly bigger shapes, neat and smooth surface, deeply cut characters, carefully filed and polished outline and inside of the Chuan, and especially standard square and roundness. Pattern of mother coins were a little bit diff erent from that of sample coins, and the reason was that, to avoid sand sticking onto coins resulted, opening of the outline was slightly round, the circumference bulged like a fi sh bone, the strokes were thinner and clear-cut in details, and the surface was bright and clean."

8.Common knife marks to Diaomu (Figure5, Figure 6)

Now that Diaomu was carved, there must have been tools for carving. What were they ? It is difficult to find out. Did they change over time ? This is also difficult to answer. However, there is a general conclusion that main tools used for carving Diaomu were at least compasses, knife, file, saw and drill. Traces of the former four tools were the most obvious and there was material evidence.

If we look at the surface of inner and outer outlines of a Diaomu, there are traces of compasses too in some Diaomu, usually at inside of the outline or outside of the inner outline.

Very deep knife marks would frequently stay at rim of the outer outline of the bottom seal. This can also be seen at rim of inner outline resembling a square. And knife marks or triangular chisel marks can often found in the bottom seal too.

At rim of a straight stroke, vertical or horizontal knife marks can be found too. These traces are regular, and most of them can not be seen with naked eye.

As for semicircular strokes, such as the character Bao in Manchu, there are irregular vertical or horizontal strokes at rim of the semicircular rou. Some strokes are quadrangular mouth-shaped or like a rectangle. Lines of the square or rectangle sink inside and form a "X" shape or two opposite "Y" shapes. They are very regular, but we do not know if the counterfeit Diaomu in period of the Republic of China were made with such rigor too.

There are also circular characters being round and shape in the inside.

So the conclusion is that, for good Diaomu, there were rules on techniques for strokes to follow when carvers made them.

9.Evolvement of techniques for Diaomu（Figure 7）

Somewhere around the evolvement of techniques for making Diaomu is quite clear for instance, the bottom seal of most QianLong Diaomu was smooth, but ever since the period of DaoGuang, few small ping Diaomu were weven, but protruding mostly.

Evolvement of strokes of Diaomu was the most remarkable, in that craftsmanship of QianLong Diaomu was incomparable with straight rims which formed an angle of almost 90° with the bottom seal and wide strokes, however, JiaQing period onwards, strokes turned to be thin, up until GuangXu period, most strokes of Diaomu were thin like silk, and rims of strokes did not form a right angle with the bottom seal, but an oblique angle instead, or even an angle of 45°. This change may be a setback in appearance, and a progress in techniques for making money by sand-casting. What is this for？ Further investigation is needed.

10.Evolvement of the character Bao in Manehu（Figure 8）

Evolvement of the character Bao in Manchu is worth discussing, especially the horizontal line opposite to the inner outline. For Diaomu in QianLong and JiaQing periods, the horizontal line of the character Bao was like, a jumping angle. In DaoGuang period, the line changed to be like an arc , with no sense of jumping, and up until XianFeng and GuangXu periods, it had a sense of roundness . This may be changes in carving techniques, but there is no relevant information. Nevertheless, if the horizontal line of the character Bao of Diaomu in QianLong and JiaQing periods was like, a jumping angle, there is a large chance that these Diaomu are carved in contemporary times. I hope to get more genuine

Diaomu of QianLong period to answer these questions.

11.Various shaping techniques for Diaomu

Each Diaomu has its own characteristics because there were various shaping techniques for Diaomu, they were carved in different times by different workers with different copper in quality, and sometimes some Diaomu were gilded and the color changed over time.

In summary, Diaomu are of various shapes, very colorful and beautiful. I have seen a QianLong Diaomu with unmatchable craftsmanship, whose strokes were deep, clear and straight, and whose bottom seal was even and smooth as a copper mirror. I have also seen a QianLong Tongbao, whose character Bao was like a lozenge , the horizontal and straight line were quite thin, the strokes was not oblique at all, and observed under an amplifier, the knife marks were straight, so the strokes gave a sense of unevenness, but on the whole, the coin was delicate and incomparable. Unfortunately, more investigations are needed to find out when it was carved and whether it was genuine.

Several small GuangXu Tongbao ping still exist today. The craftsmanship was mostly poor, with protruding bottom seal, quite a lot of knife marks, strokes thin like silk, extremely oblique stroke rim, just like a triangular file. The character Bao in Manehu had a many knife marks, which formed a positive angle with strokes. As regard to rubbing of GuangXu Diaomu, the strokes were thin like hairs, quite exquisite, but it is a pity that seen under an amplifier, the craftsmanship was coarse and there was no beauty at all. But still, the craftsmanship of some Diaomu was quite delicate.

The craftsmanship of large XianFeng money, especially large BaoYuan and BaoQuan moneyequivalent to a hundred or thousand was extremely delicate, comparable to coins carved in QianLong period. For these large coins, the bottom seal was really smooth like a mirror, all knife marks vanished and strokes were study. It is hard to put them down and they are truly King of the coins.

Most small XianFeng ping were carved in an exquisite way. Generally speaking, the strokes were thinner than those of QianLong Diaomu, but wider than GuangXu Diaomu, with oblique lines, but not as oblique as those of GuangXu Diaomu. On the back there was the character Bao in Manchu, the knife marks went along the character, different from those of GuangXu Diaomu, where the traces and lines formed a positive angle. For small XianFeng ping Diaomu, most of the bottom seals were protruding.

I believe that counterfeit XuanTong Diaomu are more than genuine ones. For XuanTong Tongbao Diaomu, at present, there are only large and small samples of small ping (baoquan), whose craftsmanship is almost the same with that of GuangXu Diaomu. However, the fake ones are more and can not be distinguished from the rubbing, rather, under an amplifier, The fake ones have unfit lines, are uneven with knife marks all over and have no sense of spirit or beauty. Please be careful.

Finally, there was a JiaQing Tongbao, the biggest horizontal lines of its character Jia were straight as they were made by a machine, but under an amplifier power 10, these long and straight horizontal lines were found out to be carved.

Nowadays, collecting and studying Diaomu is a special learning. It is relatively easy to tell genuine XianFeng and GuangXu coins from the counterfeit since they exist in abundance. There are many a QianLong Diaomu too, but even more were carved in later periods, so that fish eyes are passed off as pearls. Coins of Yongzheng, JiaQing and DaoGuang periods are even more difficult to distinguish.

The book by Mr. Ding recorded only a few Diaomu, while *Recording of Qing Money in the Palace Museum* by Huang Pengxiao recorded a great number of Diaomu, the most of which are from JiaQing, DaoGuang and XianFeng periods. Unfortunately, there are no real coins as evidence, and what was included in the book by Mr. Huang were copies instead of rubbings, so it is unable to tell whether the coins are genuine or counterfeit.

There are many literatures talked about Diaomu, which, unfortunately, were mostly rubbings, and it is difficult to decide whether they were Diaomu or mother money. Some literatures have pictures in them, but it is a pity that they are blurred and the real appearance can not be discerned.

We have stepped into a new era, and can not be careless in studying ancient money. We should call a spade a spade and make a justified explanation. Certainly, the studies and conclusions are not necessarily correct, but this is more logic than unsystematic study anyway.

The above are just several examples and I hope that quan pals at home and abroad will pay more attention on this aspect and save the research ignoring Diaomu, King of the quan.

The author thinks that Chinese Association of Ancient Money should organize teams to do some objective research on Diaomu. In this way, study on ancient money would be more interesting and reference can be provided for quan researchers of later generations.

Carving time （Table 1）

Official carving under the central government		Official carving under local authorities or private carving
Qing Dynasty	Contemporary	Contemporary
Later generations	Later generations （？）	
Republic of China	Counterfeit	Counterfeit

Procedures for casting new coins in Qing Dynasty （Table 2）

Bureau under Ministry of Revenue and Ministry of Works

Provincial money bureau

Carved by provincial money bureau on their own discretion

（Wood）Ivory sample coin

Copper pattern coin		Copper pattern coin
Initially made mother coin	Initially made mother coin （Sample coin issued by the Ministries）	Initially made mother coin
Printed mold coin	Printed mold coin	Printed mold coin （？）
Submitted sample coin	Submitted sample coin	

Figure 1　Pattern coins （Diaomu）

Figure 2　Mother coins

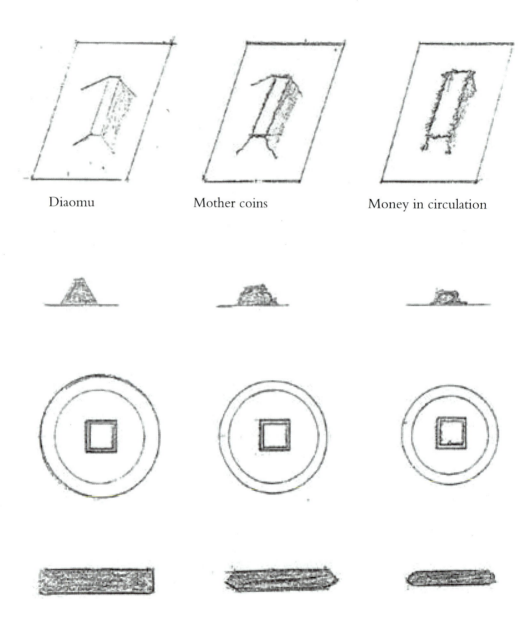

Diaomu Mother coins Money in circulation

Figure 3　Diaomu · Mother coins · Money in circulation

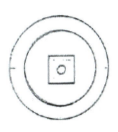
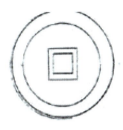
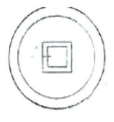

Gold mouth not opened   Initially made mother coin   Gold mouth opened

Figure 4   Evolvement of the outer outline

Diaomu

Mother coins

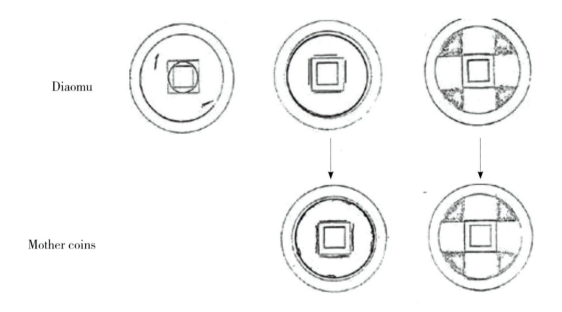

Figure 5   Knife marks or chiseling marks

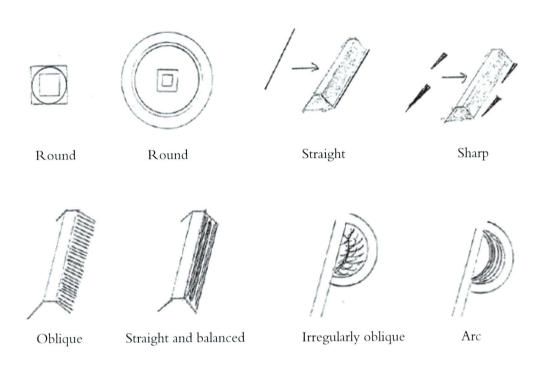

Round   Round   Straight   Sharp

Oblique   Straight and balanced   Irregularly oblique   Arc

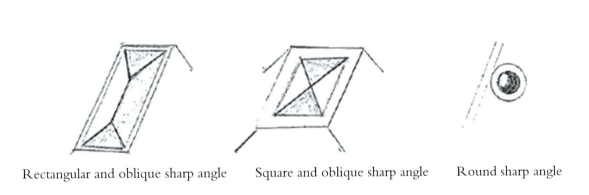

Rectangular and oblique sharp angle   Square and oblique sharp angle   Round sharp angle

Figure 6   Common knife marks to Diaomu

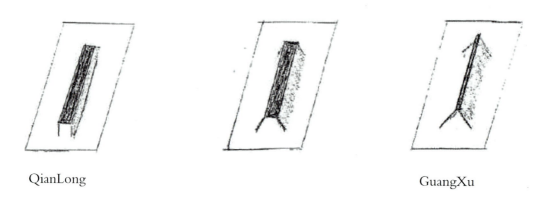

QianLong   GuangXu

Figure 7   Evolvement of techniques for carving Diaomu

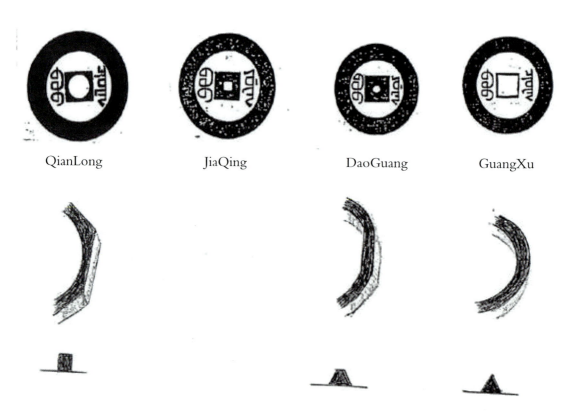

QianLong   JiaQing   DaoGuang   GuangXu

Figure 8   Evolvement of the character Bao in Manehu

雕母钱和母钱

雕母钱又称祖钱，雕的材质有铜、铅、象牙、木和石等。清代雕母以铜为主，存世比较多，象牙雕的有咸丰和光绪钱，铅的有光绪雕母。最近在中国，又发现有大元国宝铅质雕母样钱（杨成麒，中国钱币，1983年，创刊号）（图9）。又有明嘉靖通宝当十大钱（张旭华，中国钱币，1984年，第三期）（图10）。以上元代"大元国宝"直径是4.6厘米，重53.3克。"嘉靖通宝"当十铜雕母钱，质为黄铜，色泽金黄，刻工极精，重23.6克，直径4.5厘米，厚0.2厘米。张旭华先生又说："现在能见到的早至明代'万历通宝'和'崇祯通宝'雕母小平钱，清代有顺治雕母和康熙锡雕母等，为数极少。"杨成麒先生又说："明代只有万历、天启、崇祯等数品。"

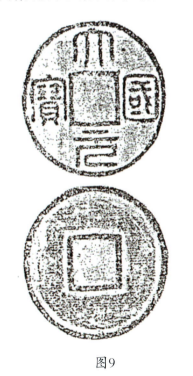

图9

图10

张旭华先生又做了下面的讨论："母钱有两种，即雕母和铸母。所谓雕母，就是用铜块、锡块或牙、木、蜡块，由刻工用刀在上面雕刻出文字和钱样来，这是最原始的钱样，俗称祖钱或雕母钱。据史书记载，在六朝后期开始用母钱法铸钱，到唐初用母钱翻砂法铸钱技术已很成熟。"

对于宋母钱，丁福保书内记载很多，尤其是铁母钱。在《中国钱币》（1983年，创刊号）高桂云先生登载一枚可称为母钱的"泰和重宝"（图11），这钱直径4.5厘米，厚0.3厘米。据杨成麒老先生说："在上海博物馆见过一两百枚泰和重宝篆文钱，均不能与此枚泰和重宝篆文钱比美。"母钱记载很多，但它们是用翻砂法铸的呢，还是用失蜡法？到现在还是一个大疑问。

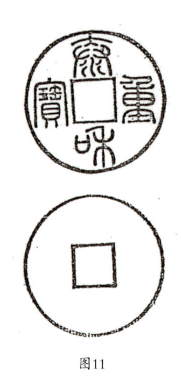

图11

《泉币》（1944年）曾登载"雍正通宝"雕母钱两枚（图12），但对雕母钱记录最多的还是黄鹏霄的《故宫清钱谱》。以前在洛杉矶差不多一枚雕母都看不到，后来陈京元先生找到两枚，这一年来我又幸运地收集到数枚（图13），才对雕母钱有了一点儿认识，图14至图17是它们的照片（由黎家驹先生拍摄）。表三中记录了它们的径长、厚度和重量，由此可见清代币制改革厉害，不像通典所说祖钱一定是10.9克，图14乾隆通宝重10.15克，图15道光通宝重7.7克，而光绪通宝只有4.11克。从雕工方面看，乾隆通宝雕工最精，结构最美。由图14至图17，以及图18的构图，我们可以看到乾隆雕母字划比较雄伟粗壮，钱肉平坦而滑，钱的边缘圆正，可是道光、光绪的钱，钱肉成弧形，边缘凸出一点儿，字划看起来像丝那么幼细，文字又不大工整。再者，我所看的二十多枚雕母，完全是黄铜雕的，没有一枚是紫铜，为什么呢？因为紫铜比黄铜容易生铜锈。再对图17光绪通宝小心观察，雕匠在雕钱时，用圆规来确定钱的内径、内廓和外廓（图19），然后再雕刻字划。如果据鲍康的《大泉图录》，钱要开金口才能铸钱，那么图14的乾隆通宝和图15的道光通宝金口未开（钱穿孔），所以是雕母钱样而未取用来铸过母钱的，这可否是真的答案，还存有疑问。

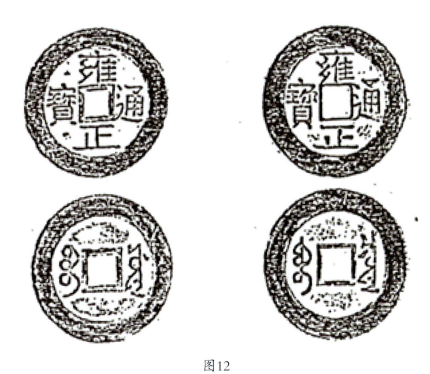

图12

图13

图14　　　　　　　图15

图16　　　　　　　图17

表三

	乾隆通宝	道光通宝	咸丰通宝	光绪通宝
径长（毫米）	26.8	25.3	36.2	23.9
厚度（毫米）	1.8	2.0	3.1	1.9
重量（克）	7.65	7.15	20.30	5.10

钱的横切面

乾隆通宝　　　　　　　　　　　　　　　　　　光绪通宝

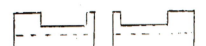 

图18

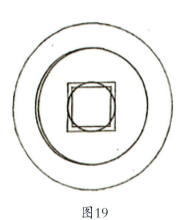

图19

常钱 母钱 常钱

图20

　　图20是两枚同样的道光通宝母钱和一枚不同范的常钱，小心研究，这两枚母钱差不多如祖钱那么漂亮，只是肉面没有那么平滑，但又不像常钱砂眼那么多，怀疑由祖钱铸母钱的方法和母钱翻砂铸常钱是有点儿不同的，我可以大胆地说它们铸制的程序一定不同，现在不能确定的是祖钱铸母钱，是否是用一种特别的翻砂法，还是用失蜡法？我认为用失蜡法比较显著。我曾做过一次失蜡铸钱的实验，当然使用失蜡法用祖钱（雕母）铸钱一定是很美的，我使用失蜡法用母钱铸钱（图21），第一次铸出来很美，研磨后亦很美，再用这种子钱（母钱铸出来的）再使用失蜡法铸钱，铸出来的钱（我叫它作孙钱）亦美，研磨后亦美，总而言之，比常钱美丽得多。以上是祖钱用失蜡法制母钱最有力的证据，望泉友指正。

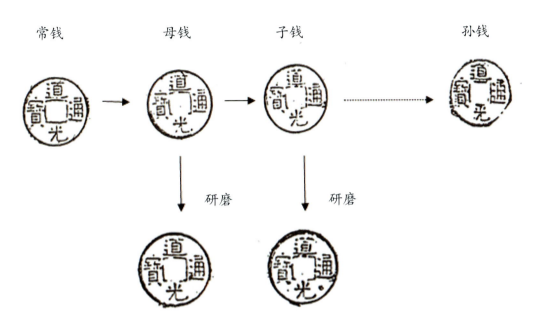

图21

DIAOMU AND MOTHER MONEY

Diaomu was also called ancestor money. It was made of copper, lead, ivory, wood and stone, etc. Diaomu in Qing Dynasty was mainly made of copper, and many still exist today, money made of ivory included XianFeng and GuangXu money, while that carved from lead included GuangXu Diaomu. Recently in China , lead dayuan guobao Diaomu sample money was discovered (Yang Chengqi, China Money, 1983, the first issue) (Figure. 9) . Besides, there were JiaJing Tongbao equivalent to ten palace coins of Ming Dynasty (Zhang Xuhua, China Money, 1984, Issue 3) (Figure. 10) . The "dayuan Tongbao" of Yuan Dynasty mentioned above are 4.6 cm in diameter, and weigh 53.3 g . "JiaJing Tongbao" equivalent to ten copper Diaomu, is made of brass, golden in color and refined in craftsmanship. It weigh 23.6 g , is 4.5 cm in diameter and 0.2 cm thick. It was also said by Mr. Zhang Xuhua said, "What exists today is just a few, including "WanLi Tongbao" and "ChongZhen Tongbao" of Ming Dynasty and ShunZhi Diaomu and tin KangXi Diaomu in Qing Dynasty" . And Yang Chengqi said, "There were only a few in WanLi, TianQi and ChongZhen periods" . It is unknown where they got the information.

Then, Zhang Xuhua made the following conclusion: there were two kinds of mother money, Diaomu and ZhuMu. Diaomu was made out of a piece of copper, tin, wood or wax with characters and samples carved in it by carvers with blades. This is the earliest sample money, commonly called ancestor money or Diaomu money. According to historical recordings, mother money was used to make money from the latter part of Six Dynasties The sand-casting technique was quite mature in the beginning years of Tang Dynasty.

As regard to mother money of Song Dynasty, a lot of information was recorded in a book by Ding, especially on iron mother money. In recent years, Gao Guiyun published a

Taihe Zhongbao, which could be called a mother money in China Money（1983, the first issue）（Figure. 11）. The money is 4.5 cm in diameter and weighs 0.3 cm . According to Mr. Yang Chengqi, more than a hundred of taihe Zhongbao money with seal characters seen in Shanghai Museum can not be compared in beauty with this Taihe Zhongbao money with seal characters. There are many recordings about mother money, but how are they made, by sand-casting or wax-losing ? This is a big question.

The magazine *Quanbi*（year 1944）once published two YongZheng Tongbao Diaomu money（Figure. 12）, but Diaomu was recorded in the largest number in *Recording of Qing Money in the Palace Museum* by Huang Pengxiao. Previously, almost no Diaomu could be seen in Los Angles, then, Chen Jingyuan found two and I encountered several Diaomu by luck（Figure. 13）. It was since then that some knowledge was accumulated on Diaomu. Figures 14 to 17 are their photos（taken by Mr. Li Jiaju on my behalf）, and table 1 is about their weight, thickness and diameter. Gains and losses in the reform of money system in Qing Dynasty can be seen from table 3. Unlike what was said in Tongdian that ancestor money was 10.9g, QianLong Tongbao in Figure 14 weighed 10.15g, DaoGuang Tongbao in Figure 15 weighed 7.7g, while GuangXu Tongbao was only 4.11g. Judged from craftsmanship, QianLong Tongbao was the most delicate and most refined in structure, whereas GuangXu Tongbao was just the opposite. It can be seen from Figures 14 to 17 and Figure 18 that strokes of characters in QianLong Diaomu was imposing and bold, the rou was plain and smooth ,and the rim round and regular, while in DaoGuang's and GuangXu's period swfaco of money, the shape of money was arc and its characters were not quite neat. Apart from that, the Diaomu I have looked at, more than twenty of them, were all made of brass, instead of purple copper. Why ? The reason is that purple copper tends to get rusted easier than brass. Then, if we look at the GuangXu Tongbao in fugure 17 carefully, when carving the money, the carvers decided the inner diameter, inner outline and outer outline using a compass （Figure, 19）, and made the strokes. According to dayuan Tulu by Bao Kang, if money could be used to make money only after the gold mouth was opened, and the god mouths of QianLong Tongbao and GuangXu Tongbao were not opened（no hole through）, so they were sample Diaomu which were not used to make mother money. It is not sure if this is the right answer.

Figure 20 are two identical DaoGuang Tongbao mother money and one regular money of different mold. If studied carefully, the two mother coins are almost as beautiful as an ancestor coin, only the swface of money is not very smooth, but the sand holes are less than those of regular coins. The doubt is that the method of making mother money using ancestor money and the method of making regular money with mother money by sand casting are different with each other. I am quite certain that their making procedures are different. Now it is impossible to decide whether mother money was made with ancestor money by a special sand-casting method or the wax-losing method. I believe that it is probably the latter. I have done an experiment on making money by wax-losing. Of course, the money must be beautiful when it is made after ancestor money (Diaomu) by the wax-losing method. I made money after mother money by wax-losing (Figure. 21), it was beautiful when it was made and polished. Then, I made money after the son money (made after the mother money). The money resulted (I called it grandson money) was beautiful too, and remained beautiful after polishing. In a word, it was a lot more beautiful than the regular. What is said above is the strongest evidence that mother money was made after ancestor money by wax-losing and I hope to get ideas from quan pals.

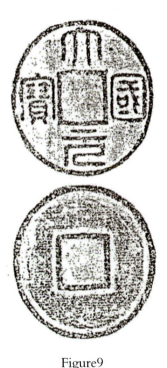

Figure9

Figure10

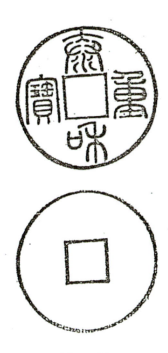

Figure11

Figure12

Figure13

Figure14   Figure15

Figure16   Figure17

Table 3

	QianLong Tongbao	DaoGuang Tongbao	XianFeng Tongbao	GuangXu Tongbao
Diameter（mm）	26.8	25.3	36.2	23.9
Thickness（mm）	1.8	2.0	3.1	1.9
Weight（g）	7.65	7.15	20.30	5.10

Cross-section of money

QianLong Tongbao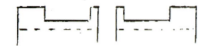

GuangXu Tongbao

Figure18

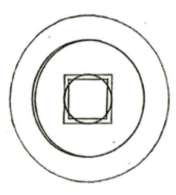

Figure19

Regular money   Mother money   Regular money

Figure20

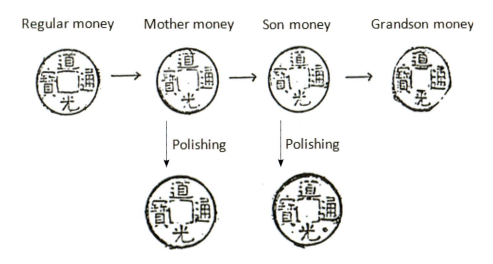

Figure21

未开金口的钱币——母钱或样钱？

有些藏家认为没有开金口的钱，一定是雕母，可是从文献和实物中已证明，清代有用雕母直接铸钱先例。所以藏家要小心未开金口而又漂亮的钱币，可以是铸出来的，是样钱或是母钱。（图22、图23）

图22　　　　　　　　　　　　　图23

未开金口的母钱

A COIN WITHOUT OPENING ITS GOLDEN MOUTH—— MOTHER COIN OR SAMPLE COIN?

Some collectors believe that a coin without opening its golden mouth（the square hole was called golden mouth by the authority of Qing Dynasty）must be a Diaomu, however, it is a pity that it has demonstrated in literature and in reality that sometimes coins were made directly after Diaomu in Qing Dynasty. As a consequence, collectors should be careful that a coin, which does not open its golden mouth and is beautiful, may be molded after other coins, and opinions differ on whether it is a sample coin or a mother coin.（See below）

A coin without opening its golden mouth

Figure22   Figure23

各种伪造雕母的方法

现代常见的制造赝品的方法不外乎以下数种：

一、改刻——常见的赝品雕母，通常多用品相好的钱或母钱改刻，藏家只要用放大镜细察，就可以见到纵横无序的刀痕，文字线条不工整，又没有神，钱面凹凸不平，又很难拓出好的拓本。（图 24）

二、翻砂或失蜡法——通常用雕母、母钱或其他为范，用失蜡法或翻砂法铸出赝品，再加工研磨钱肉，市面上见的通常是大钱，不留心看会以为是真雕母，但仔细看，铜质通常是暗而无光，在肉和字划之间用放大镜看，可以看出很多砂眼，再细观察，亦可找出流铜的痕迹。（图 25）

三、机器雕铸和人工雕铸——清末民初，前清的雕刻工匠曾雕铸过赝品雕母，这种雕母和真雕母泛有两样，只是在铜质上逊于真品。二十多年前，传说有人曾雕铸过赝品雕母，据说很逼真。近年市面上曾出现机器打造的雕母，但铜质很劣，文字劣而不雅，一看便知不是真雕母。至于伪雕的雕母，孙仲汇在《中国古钱鉴赏与收藏》一书中（上海书店出版社，44 ~ 46 篇）曾做下面的叙述。

"河北某地，有人出自刻铜世家，自 1990 年至今，利用旧铜材料刻了近千枚雕母，初出时骗倒了一大批收藏家，后期所刻水平更高，但泉币界对此已有警惕，所以为害不及早期，闻近年遭车祸，又年事日高，作品少多了，但南方却有人无师自通，步此公后尘。"本书作者没遇到过上面所述的假雕母，所以没法提出任何意见或疑问。（图 26、图 27（a）（b））

四、镶嵌——曾见用人工锯锉出古钱的每一个字，又锯制出四方的内廓和圆的外廓，最后镶嵌在一片比例正确的圆的金属片上，完成了一个美丽的古钱，几可跟真雕母媲美，可惜是赝品。

五、纯出臆造——这是造假中伎俩最拙劣的一种。由于造假之人异想天开，毫无根据，做工亦极粗糙，较易辨别。尤其是咸丰钱臆造伪品层出不穷。由于有的咸丰伪钱钱文借范于样钱版子，再造出一大批稀奇古怪的出谱品，铸工又颇精，以至于还被误认为是新发现的样钱，所以各位收藏家一定要小心。

当然，其他造假之手法还有多种，且技艺不断改进，即使此道老手，恐亦难免不上其当。

图24 改刻

图25 失蜡法

图26 机雕

图27（a）机器雕母（面）

图27（b）机器雕母（底）

METHODS FOR FORGING DIAOMU

Diaomu were mostly made in Qing Dynasty. Common modern methods for making counterfeit Diaomu are mainly as the following:

Ⅰ. Re-carving – Commonly-seen counterfeit Diaomu are usually re-carved from good-looking coins or mother coins. Under an amplifier, the collector may see cut marks in disorder, unneat characters and lines and no spirit. Besides, the coin surface is uneven, difficult to produce good rubbing. (Figure 24)

Ⅱ. Sand-casting or wax-losing – Counterfeits are usually made after Diaomu, mother coins or other ones with sand-casting or wax-losing method, and then polished in the surface part. What circulate in the market are large coins, which may be mistaken for Diaomu at first glance, however, when observed carefully, the cooper is dim and dark, and seen under an amplifier, there are many sand holes between the Rou and strokes of the characters, and traces of copper flow can also be found if observed more carefully. (Figure 25)

Ⅲ. Mechanic casting and manual casting – During later Qing Dynasty and Early Republic of China, carvers of the Qing Dynasty has carved and casted counterfeit Diaomu, which looks almost the same as genuine Diaomu, except that it is inferior in the cooper used. It is said like that a decade ago, someone made counterfeit Diaomu that were almost real ones. Diaomu casted by machine present themselves on the market in recent years, only with cooper of poor quality and ugly-looking characters, and known to be counterfeit at first sight. As regard to falsely made Diaomu, Song Zhonghui wrote in the book *Appreciation and Collection of Ancient Chinese Money* (Chapter 44~46, Shanghai bookstore publishing house) that, "Someplace in Hebei province, there was a person born from a family that had been doing copper carving for generations. He had made almost a thousand Diaomu out of old cooper materials since 1990s. Initially he got a lot of collectors fooled and was even more skilled later. But the ancient money community was alerted and the lasing was not as much as before. It was said that the production was low as he is old and got an accident recently. However, there are Southerners who are self-learned make fake money." The author has not encountered with the fake Diaomu mentioned above, and can put forward no opinions or questions. (Figure 26, Figure27 (a) (b))

IV. Inlaying – I have seen that a person filed each character of an ancient coin, then the square hole and the round outline, and inlay it finally in a round metal with perfect proportionality. Finally, a beautiful ancient coin was created almost like genuine Diaomu. It is, unfortunately, a counterfeit.

V. Out of pure imagination – This is the poorest in all of the forging tricks. The work is coarse and distinguishable because the forger make fake money only by his imagination without any accordings too far. Particularly, fake XianFeng products emerged one after another. Some of the fake XianFeng coins are odd out-of-catalogue (Chupu) products made after sample coins. They are so delicately that they are thought as sample coins newly discovered. Collectors should be aware of this.

Certainly, there are many other forging ways, and as the tricks get improved over time, even one with rich experience may swallow the bait.

Figure24　Re-carving

Figure25   Lost Wax Method

Figure26   Machine Made

Figure27（a） Machine Made Ancestor Coin（Front）

Figure27（b） Machine Made Ancestor Coin（Bottom）

中国古钱的特色

中国的钱币起源甚早，已有数千年的历史。古钱犹如一面明镜，能映出民族的智慧，朝代的兴衰，又涉及社会、文化、经济、民生、艺术等各个领域。

中国古钱有多个特点：

一、有悠久的历史。正如中国的"铜具"始于商汤时代，古钱大约出现在公元前一千多年，比欧洲最古老的钱币早三四百年。

二、古钱有独立的发展。方孔钱是中国人特有的发明，其方孔可以用方条串起，便于研磨其外廓。方孔钱又可以体现出中国"天圆地方"的哲理思想。

三、古钱继承有序。西方各国，一旦改朝换代，钱币便会被销毁；而中国方孔钱的形制，在秦汉以后，即便改朝换代，其形制仍保持原貌。如五铢钱沿用了七百多年，而唐朝开元通宝一直用到明末清初，还在市场上流通。

四、古钱形制完美。中国古钱的造型非常简单，用"天圆地方"的概念，加上文字，配以极简的轮廓构成。正如蔡养吾先生所说："由于文字结构的完美，诱导出卓越的书法，复借书法的卓越，造成极高度的钱币艺术，既能表现出我们民族的优秀风格，又能流露出不同的时代精神。"正如秦汉用小篆，王莽创出"玉筋篆"和"悬针篆"，唐有八分书，而宋又有"三体钱"和"瘦金体"。

FEATURES OF ANCIENT CHINESE COINS

I . A long history: Just like Chinese "bronze tool" appeared under Tang's reign of Shang Dynasty, in over a thousand of years B.C., three to four hundred years earlier than the oldest coin in Europe.

II . Independent development: square-holed coin was a special invention by Chinese people. The coins could be strung together with a square stick through their square holes, allowing for rubbing of the outline. Besides, square-holed coin represents the Chinese philosophy of "round sky and square earth".

III . Sequence in succession: In Western countries, once an old dynasty was replaced with a new one, its money would be destroyed, whereas in China , the shape of square-holed coins remained unchanged after Qin and Han Dynasties in spite of dynasty changes. For instance, Wuzhu money lasted for over 700 years, and Kaiyuan Tongbao of Tang Dynasty was still in use until later Ming Dynasty and early Qing Dynasty.

IV. Perfect shape: Shape of ancient Chinese coins was very simple. It was based on the idea of "round sky and square earth" , engraved with characters and molded in a fairly simple outline. Just like what was said Cai Yangwu Perfection of the structure of characters gives rise to excellent calligraphy, which in turn contributes to money art of a very high level, representing the distinctive style of our nation and spirits of different times, as is the case Xiaozhuan was used in Qin and Han Dynasties, Wang Mang created Yujinzhuan and Xuanzhenzhuan, Bafenshu was popular in Tang Dynasty and Santiqian and Shoujinti were unique in Song Dynasty.

中国铸钱的阶段

中国古代钱币的铸造大概可以分为子范（土、石、铜子范）、母范（砖铜）和翻砂法三个阶段。

第一个阶段，是用阴文子范（泥陶质、石质或铜质）直接铸钱。

第二个阶段，是用阳文母范（砖或铜）印制泥子范，然后用子范铸钱。

第三个阶段，是用母钱翻砂法铸钱。其法先做"样钱"或"祖钱"，再依祖钱做出"母钱"，鼓铸时，如明朝宋应星所写的《天工开物》内所描述："凡铸钱模以木四条为空框'木长一尺二寸，阔一寸二分'。土炭末筛令极细填实框中。微洒杉木炭灰或柳木炭灰于其面上，或熏模则用松香与清油。然后以母钱百文，'用锡雕成'或字或背布置其上。又用一框如前法填实合盖之。既合之后，已成面、背两框，随手覆转，则母钱尽落后框之上。又用一框填实，合上后框，如是转覆，只合十余框，然后以绳捆定。其木框上弦原留入铜眼孔，铸工用鹰嘴钳，洪炉提出熔罐。一人以别钳扶抬罐底相助，逐一倾入孔中。冷定解绳开框，则磊落百文如花果附枝。模中原印空梗，走铜如树枝样，夹出逐一摘断，以待磨锉成钱。凡钱先锉边沿儿，以竹木条直贯数百文受锉，后锉平面则逐一为之。"

这种方法又称为翻砂法。虽具有土范与铜范两种方法的优点，却也有难以避免的缺憾。

一、如在倒换木框时，使母钱受到震动，发生滑走移位的情形，便会在砂上印成两个印模，使文字便成双画，或使轮廓不能周正。这种现象名之为"走范"。

二、如若合范时未使两范对正，铸出钱来，面背之间便出现偏差，名曰"错范"。

三、若两框接合不密，使多余的熔铜留于模内，成钱后，面上有铜块如瘤，或轮侧穿内有铜片若翼，则名之曰"漏范"。

四、若印模欠佳，沟道壅阻，注铜时，熔浆不能遍满模内，有孔洞出现，则名之曰"失范"。

因此，钱币铸成之后，从钱枝上剪下来，必须滚锉磨洗，才能周正。明朝以后，为使钱币美观，除了赤仄涂炭之外，又创出"火漆""金背"两种方法。所谓火漆法是在铜钱上涂以豆油，放在炭火上炙烤，久之钱面上就变得乌黑发亮，犹若珐琅一般。所谓金背法，是把铜钱烤热，涂以明矾水，冷却即可变成黄金一般，闪灼发亮。翻砂法的优点，是适于大量生产。

STAGES OF COIN-CASTING IN CHINA

Coin-casting in ancient China fall roughly into three stages: Zifan secondary mold (earth, stone, copper secondary mold), Mufan mother mold (brick copper) and sand casting method.

Stage 1, casting coins directly to secondary mold (earthen, stone or copper mold) with characters cut in intaglio.

Stage 2, making earthen secondary mold to mother mold (brick or copper mold) with characters cut in relief and then casting money with the secondary mold.

Stage 3, casting coins with method of sand casting to mother mold. That is, first, make "sample coin" or "ancestor coin", after which "mother coin" is made. While minting coins by melting metals, as was said in *Tiangong Kaiwu* by Song Yingxing of Ming Dynasty, "To make coin mold, 4 wooden sticks are made into a frame (the stick is 12 cun in length and 1.2 cun in width). Screen the coal powder and fill the extremely fine powder into the frame. Scatter a little of fir or willow charcoal on the surface, or use rosin and boiled oil to make smoking mold. Then, a hundred mother coins (carved with tin), front or back, are placed on it. Another frame is filled and covered as described above. After joining with each other, there are two frames, front and back. Turn it over, the mother coins fall in the frame behind. Then another frame is filled and joins with the frame. This is repeated and more than ten frames are joined, and then tied together with a rope. There are holes on upper rim of the wooden frame for copper to be filled and molders will pick out the fusion pot from a great furnace with eagle's beak pliers. Another man will help by lifting bottom of the furnace with another plier and pour fused copper inside into the holes. When it cools, release the robe and open the frames, then a hundred of coins are there like fruits on a branch. Initially there are empty stems impressed in the mold, with copper running like a branch. Take the stem out with scissors and pick off the raw coins to be polished. First, as regards polishing the rim of a coin, hundreds of coins are strung together with a bamboo stick and polished all at once. When it comes to polish the planes, the coins are done one by one."

This method is also called sand-casting. Although having advantages of both earthen and copper molds, it has also unavoidable disadvantages.

Ⅰ. If the mother coins are shaken and transposed while overturning the frames, two impressions will appear on the sand, making the characters to be double or the outline to be irregular. This phenomenon is called "out of mold".

Ⅱ. If two molds are not properly against each other, the coins produced will have discrepancy between the front and back. This is called "mold".

Ⅲ. If two frames are not tightly joined and excessive fused copper remains in the mold, the coins will have copper lumps like tumors on the surface, or thin copper pieces like wings in the lateral Chuan of the ring. This is called "leakage of mold".

Ⅳ. If the impression is not good with blocked channels, then during the process of pouring copper, the fused liquid can not fill the mold, resulting in holes. This is called "lost of mold".

Therefore, after the coins are casted, take them from the branch with scissors, and roll, file, rub and wash them to make them well-shaped as possible. Since Ming Dynasty, two methods of "sealing wax" and "coating with gold on the back" have been invented apart from Chize filing and glowing and Tutan to make coins more pleasing to the eye. The so-called "sealing wax" refers to the method that a copper coin, with bean oil applied on it, is roasted on charcoal fire, until it becomes dark and shiny, just like enamel, while the "coating with gold on the back" method is that a copper coin is heated and coated with alum water, and looks like glittering gold after cooling.The sand-casting method is advantageous in which it allows for mass production.

钱制与钱法的疑问

中国铸钱，秦汉以前用石、铜和泥范，隋唐以后，翻砂铸钱，可惜记载不多，独明代宋应星对翻砂程序，记述颇详。

在《古泉》一书，宋有铁母泉，明清有雕母，可惜唐、宋、元各朝，雕母记载全无。

丁福保《古钱大辞典》记载北宋、南宋铁母多枚，清钱雕母若干枚，可惜对它们没有做详细讨论。至于母钱拓本，有最多记载的是黄鹏霄的《故宫清钱谱》，他把清钱分类为祖、母、样、常和大钱多种。

前人记载祖钱是雕成的，雕钱中有小孔，或圆或方，像丁福保所说的雕母，雕钱一经采用，中央小孔便被锉大成方孔，便成祖钱。所以丁福保所录的没有大方孔的雕母，或许是不被采用或被淘汰的祖钱前身。

黄鹏霄引通考："凡铸钱之法，先将净铜錾凿成二钱三分者约祖钱，随铸造一钱六七分不等约母钱，然后即铸制钱，每遇更定钱制，例先将钱式进呈，其直省开局之始，亦例由户局先铸祖钱、母钱及制钱各一文，颁发各省，令照式鼓铸。"

再看黄鹏霄记载的从乾隆到光绪时的祖钱，大小不一，直径大的 3 厘米，而小的，2.2 厘米。这样看来，祖钱的重量不一定是两钱三分（大约是 11.5 克）。我曾见过光绪雕母只有一钱二分（5.6 克）。

到现在，我还是不明白祖、母、样、常、大各种钱之间的关系。图 28 是它们之间的互相关系，图 29 选自黄鹏霄《故宫清钱谱》，除图 28 可引证祖、母、样有直接的关系外，其他祖和大或常，母和大或常的关系，还是混淆不清。至今为止，我还不知道在哪里下功夫才可以找到答案，望泉友提供意见。

图28

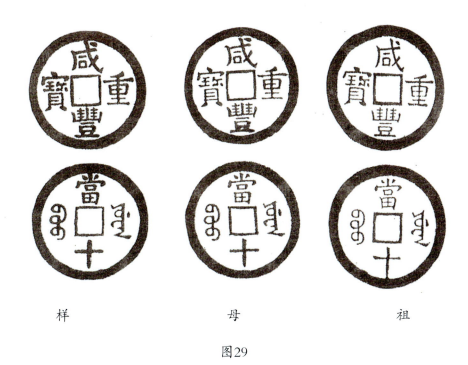

图29

　　最近花了一点儿工夫，将钱做了浅显的解剖，我认为这样才可以认识母钱和样钱的分别。图30是"钱"的立体坐标图，从立体坐标图便可以得到各部位的视图，分析各部位的视图才明白母钱、样钱和常钱的奥秘。

　　图31可看出钱径的改变，用翻砂铸钱，内径因金属冷却收缩缘故，所以径长渐减，外廓因金属收缩和铸钱后磨边，外廓的宽度亦渐渐减少，但内廓却成反比，如果不经人工锉修，内廓的宽度会越变越宽。

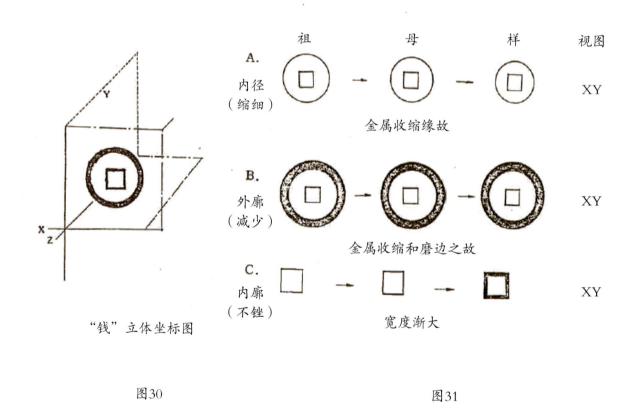

"钱"立体坐标图

图30

图31

　　图32是方孔钱部位的横切面，由这些部位视图便可以了解线条高度，从祖钱到样钱，高度会逐渐降级，而线条的角度会逐渐增大，外廓径的宽度会减少（磨边之故），其厚度会渐薄，祖样钱的边沿儿平滑，母钱边沿儿比较圆凸，这是不是和铸钱树（枝）有关呢?

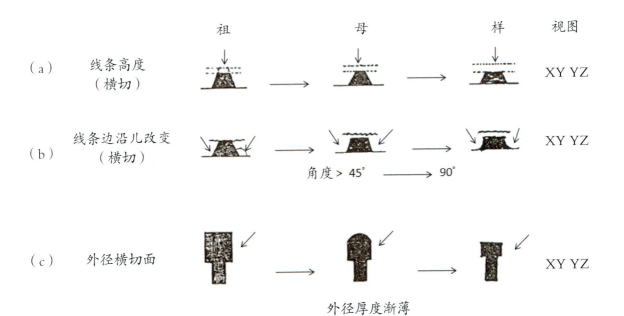

图32

图 33 是古钱的纵横切面图视图，祖钱的钱面或钱背的盘地是因祖钱雕刻后，钱的盘地是打磨平滑的，不像母钱或样钱翻砂，所以盘地越变越会粗凸不平，见图 33（a）。又从肉廓切面见图 33（b），祖钱的字划比样钱幼细得多，如果雕匠功夫不够或一不小心，字条会太狭或有点儿凹凸不平之感（尤其是小平钱），至于母钱字划比较圆滑不整，这是母钱翻砂（或蜡模）后，没有研磨之故，但常钱却不然，铸钱后，常钱要经过研磨，所以通考卷十六有说："每炉额设炉头一人，其所需工价有八行匠役：曰看火匠，曰翻砂匠，曰刷灰匠，曰染作匠，曰剉边匠，曰滚边匠，曰磨钱匠，曰洗眼匠……"。

图 33（c）的视图是对外廓内缘斜角的分析，所以斜角由工整逐渐变为不工整（翻砂的缘故）。

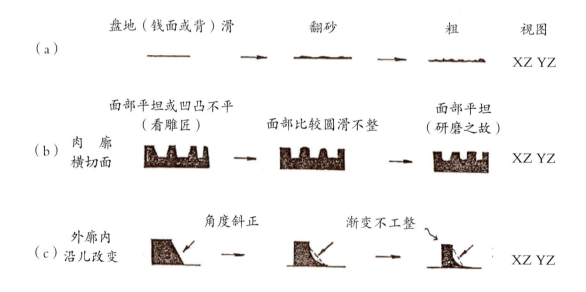

图33

图 34 是祖、母、样、常等线条、字体和点
划的改变。如图 34（a），线条由幼线条变为凹
凸不平的字划，图 34（b）的王字下划右挑，但
翻砂后的样钱大多都模糊不清楚，图 34（c）的
点形改变亦是如此，由明晰的点划变为圆不圆、
尖不尖的字划。

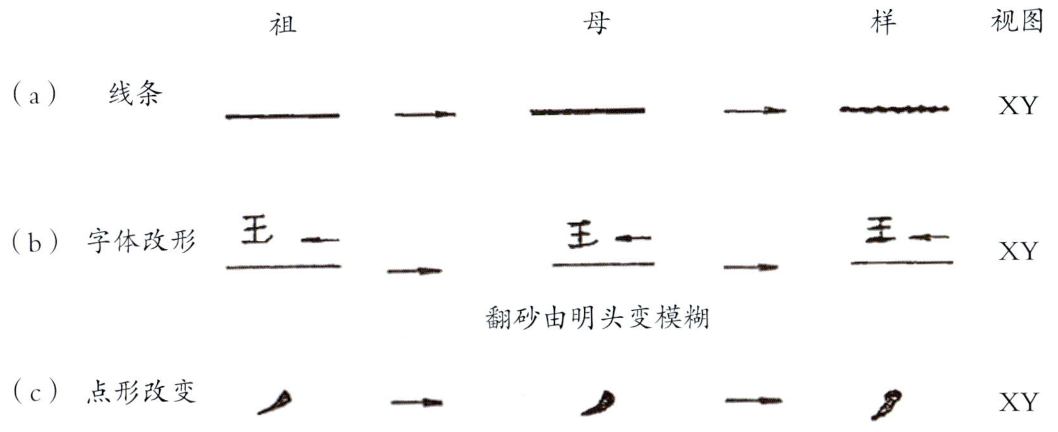

		祖		母		样	视图
（a）	线条	——	→	——	→	～～	XY
（b）	字体改形	王	→	王	→	王	XY
			翻砂由明头变模糊				
（c）	点形改变		→		→		XY

图34

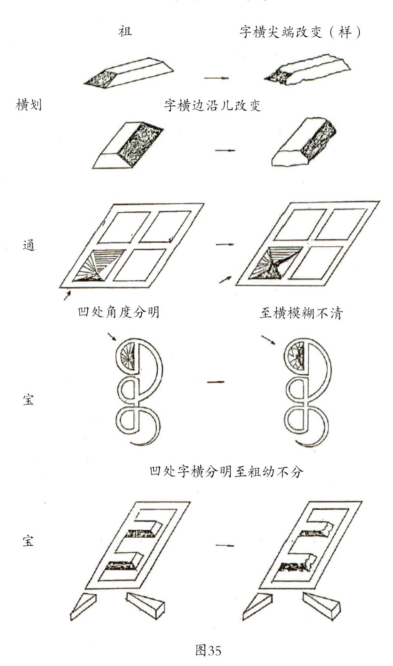

翻砂字划改变立体图

图35

图35是翻砂字划改变的立体图，这里不用详细解释，看图便可以明了各种改变。

综上可见，祖、母、样、常钱的改变，字由清晰变模糊，字划由小变大，外廓由宽变狭，内廓由狭变宽，径由大而小，厚度由厚而薄，量由重而轻，钱面由平滑变为凹凸不平（翻砂），角度由明显而改为不正，铜质合金亦做不同的改变。以上浅见，望泉坛好友指正。

QUESTIONS ON MONEY–MAKING MECHANISM AND MONEY–MAKING METHODS

In China, money was made after stone, copper or earth mold before Qin and Han Dynasties. It was made by sand-casting after Sui and Tang Dynasties, but unfortunately there were few recordings about this, only that Song Yingxing of Ming Dynasty described in detail the sand-casting procedure.

In books about *Ancient Quan*, there were iron mother quan of Song Dynasty, Diaomu in Ming and Qing Dynasties, while there was no recordings of Diaomu in Tang, Song or Yuan Dynasties. (Note: It was said that there were a JiaJing Tongbao equivalent to ten liang of Diaomu in a museum. And a lead DaYuan guobao Diaomu money.)

Ding Fubao wrote about many iron mother coins of North and South Song Dynasties and several Diaomu of Qing Dynasty in Dictionary on Ancient Money, but it is a pity that he did not discuss it in detail. As for rubbing of mother money, it was recorded in the largest number in Recording of Qing *Money in the Palace Museum* by Huang Pengxiao, who classified coins into several types, ancestor coin, mother coin, sample coin, common coin and palace coin. It was recorded earlier that ancestor money was carved, with a small hole in the center, round or square. Just like what was said about by Ding Fubao, once Diaomu was used, the small hole in the center was made into a large hole, and became ancestor money. Therefore, the coins recorded by Ding Fubao included no Diaomu with big square holes, or predecessor ancestor coins that were not used or fell into disuse.

Huang Pengxiao quoted Tongkao that, "In all methods for making money, pure copper was made into ancestor money of two qian and three fen, then mother money of one qian and six or seven fen, then money. Whenever the money-making mechanism was modified, the money patterns were submitted in the first place, starting from the directly supervising bureau. As a rule, the bureau made each one of ancestor coin, mother coin and molded coin and distributed them for each province to make money after."

Then, looked at ancestor coins recorded by Huang from QianLong period to GuangXu period. the coins are in different sizes, ranging from 2.2cm to 3cm. Seen from this, weight of ancestor money was not necessarily two qian and three fen (approximately 11.5g). I have seen a GuangXu Diaomu that is only one qian and two fen (5.6g).

Up until now I still do not know the relationship among ancestor money, mother money, sample money, common money and palace money. Figure 28 is a drawing about their relationship, and Figure 29 is adapted from *Recording of Qing Money in the Palace Museum* by Huang Pengxiao. Apart from Figure 28, which could be quoted that there was a direct relationship among ancestor money, mother money and sample money. The relationship among ancestor money, palace money and common money and that anong mother, palace among money and common money are confused with each other. Till today, I still have no idea where to find the answer.

Lately I have spent some time on investigation of money. only that, I think, can we tell the difference between mother and sample money. Figure 30 is stereo-coordinate graph of money, from which we can see the view of each part. Analysis of view of each part can help find out the secret of mother, sample and common money.

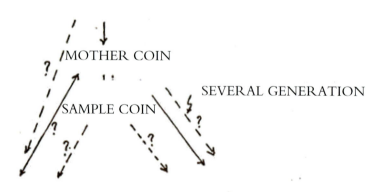

Figure 28

Changes to the diameter of money can be seen from Figure 31. When a coin was made by sand-casting, the inner diameter shrank due to cooling of metal, so the diameter decreased. The outer outline became narrower than before because of metal shrank and rim polishing. But the contrary happened to the inner outline. If there was no artificial manual polishing, the inner outline would get wider and wider.

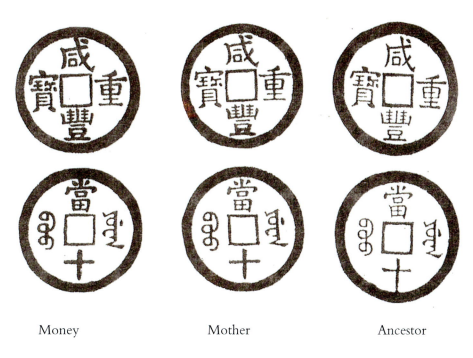

| Money | Mother | Ancestor |

Figure 29

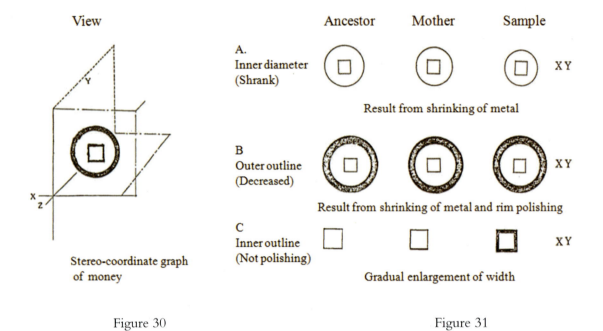

View

Stereo-coordinate graph
of money

Figure 30

Ancestor   Mother   Sample

A.
Inner diameter
(Shrank)   X Y

Result from shrinking of metal

B
Outer outline
(Decreased)   X Y

Result from shrinking of metal and rim polishing

C
Inner outline
(Not polishing)   X Y

Gradual enlargement of width

Figure 31

Figure 32 is crossing sections of coins with square holes, from which it can be seen that from ancestor money to sample money, height of the lines decreased, while their angles became larger, so that the width was less (due to rim polished) , the thickness became less, and the rim of ancestor money was smooth, while that of mother money was rather uneven. Is this relevant to the money-making tree (branch) ?

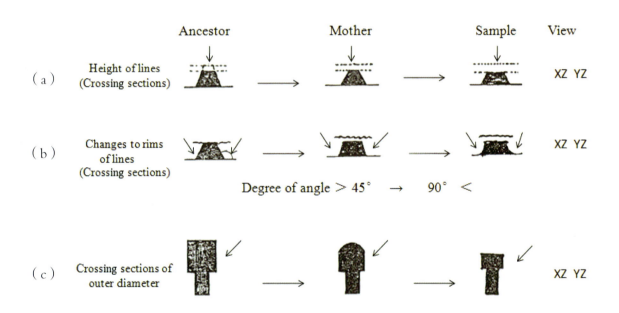

Thickness of inner diameter became less
Rims of outer diameter of ancestor money were smooth
Rims of mother money were rather round and protruding

Figure 32

Figure 33 is longitudinal and crossing sections of ancient money. Appearance of front or back of ancestor money was polished to be smooth after the money was made, unlike that in sand-casting of mother or sample money, which became uneven Figure. 33（a）. Seen from the crossing sections of the surface outline Figure. 33（b）, characters of ancestor money felt a little bit uneven（especially small ping money）, and those of mother money were quite smoothly untidy, which was because the money was not polished after sand-casting（or wax-molding）, but this was not the case of common money. After a common coin was made, it went through the polishing procedure. It was said in Tongkao volume 16 that, "each stove was managed by a man, who needed workers for 8 kinds of process, taking care of the fire, sand-casting, ash brushing, dyeing, rim polishing, rim rolling and hole washing..." . View of Figure 33（c）is analysis of oblique angles of inner rim of the outer outline, so the oblique angles changed from being tidy to being untidy.（Note: result of sand-casting）Figure 34 is the changes to lines, character styles and point strokes of ancestor, mother, sample and common money. In Figure 34（a）, the lines changed from thin lines into uneven strokes, and in Figure 34（b）, the last stroke of the character "王" swung to the right. But those of sample money after sand-casting were mostly blurred, so were changes to points in Figure 34（c）, where the point stroke was changed to a stroke that could not be spoken of in terms of roundness or sharpness.

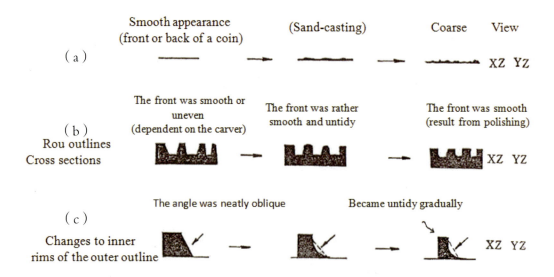

Figure 33

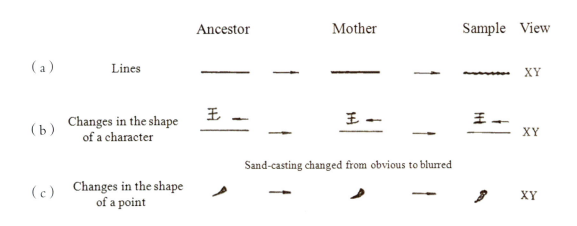

Figure 34

Figure 35 is the stereograph of changes to sand-casting strokes. Detailed explanation is not necessary now and various changes can be seen from the graph.

The following changes to ancestor, mother, sample and common money can be seen from the above: the characters changed from clear to blurred, strokes from the small to the big, outer outline from the wide to the narrow, inner outline from the narrow to the wide, diameter from the big to the small, thickness from the thick to the thin, weight from the heavy to the light, surface of the money from the smooth to the uneven (sand-casting), angle from the obvious to the oblique and copper alloy changed as well. I hope quan pals would make corrections to the opinions above.

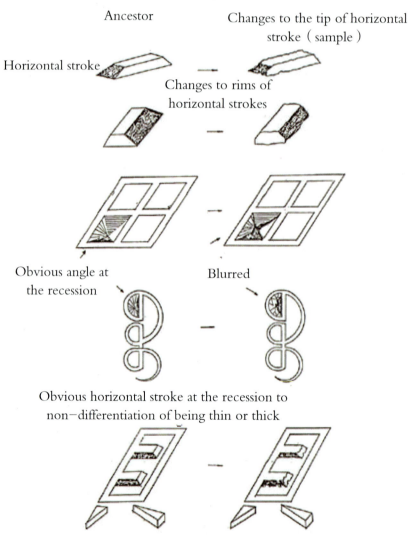

Stereograph of changes to sand-casting strokes

Ancestor

Changes to the tip of horizontal stroke（sample）

Horizontal stroke

Changes to rims of horizontal strokes

Obvious angle at the recession

Blurred

Obvious horizontal stroke at the recession to non-differentiation of being thin or thick

Figure 35

钱各部的名称

　　虽然方孔钱设计简单，但由于流通广泛，多被藏家收集。而钱各部分亦有其名称，钱的铜质部分称为"肉"，有厚薄之分。中间的孔各为"穿"或"好"，大穿称为"广穿"，狭小的名为"窄穿"。穿上方的铜质部分为"穿上"，下方为"穿下"，左右两方各为"穿左"及"穿右"。

式型不同的轮

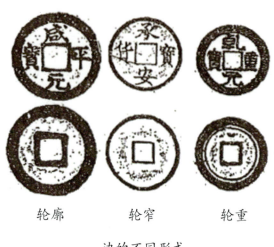

轮廓　　　　轮窄　　　　轮重

边的不同形式

镟剉　　平夷　　平夷　　隐起

图36

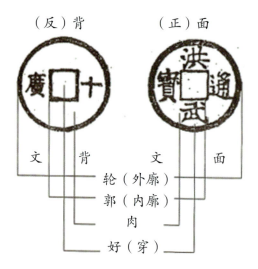

图37

NAMES OF PARTS OF A SQUARE-HOLED COIN

Although the square-holed coin is simple in design, due to extensive currency, it is collected by collectors. Each part of it has its own name. Copper part of the coin is called "rou", either thick or thin. The hole in the middle is "Chuan" or "hao", with the large Chuan called "wide Chuan" and the small Chuan "narrow Chuan". Copper part that above Chuan is "Chuan-above", that below is "Chuan-below", while left and right to it are called "Chuan-left" and "Chuan-right" respectively.

Rings of Different Types

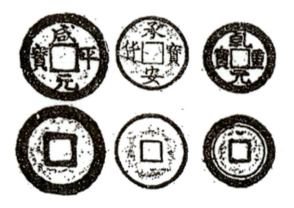

Wing Ring   Narrow Ring   Double Ring

Rings of Different Type

File   Flat   Slanting Indistinct

Figure 36

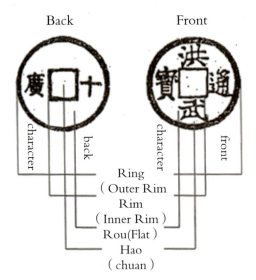

Back   Front

character   back   character   front

Ring
(Outer Rim
Rim
(Inner Rim)
Rou(Flat)
Hao
(chuan)

Figure 37

鉴定

研究雕母，鉴别其真假，亦像其他古钱一样以文、质、声、色、味、神为基础，然后是"断年代""觅出处"和"别品制"等事项。研究雕母，最重要的要看其雕工。

鉴定雕母工作，通常由以下各方面着手，兹分述如下：

一、辨质——雕母通常是用最精炼的铜来雕刻的，所以不能有砂眼，铜质通常是呈光亮的金黄色，当然亦有许多例外。

二、验工——雕母是用刀或其他工具雕的，所以在钱面上每一划都很明显，字一定是秀丽、雄壮和有神气的，用放大镜看，通常可以看见刀痕，而且字的笔锋生动。雕母不可能有流铜或错范的现象。

三、重量——雕母一定比由它所铸出来的母钱或样钱大些、重些和厚些，雕母在手中有重而实的感觉。

四、观色——雕母很少有锈或铜绿的，雕母是精铜造的，其色金黄而有古朴的感觉。所谓"黑漆古"和"水银古"，在雕母钱中几乎找不到。有些雕母呈现光亮如镜的感觉，大概是一枚雕母在未雕之前，其铜块原料曾被打磨过的缘由吧。

在鉴定雕母的过程中，闻气味（不能有酸性味道），看拓本（拓出的拓本要有神）等，也都是鉴定雕母真假的方法。

AUTHENTICATION

Authentication of the genuine and counterfeit in the study of Diaomu, just like that of other ancient coins, is based on character, texture, sound, color, smell and spirit, and then factors like "determining the time", "looking for the source" and "differentiating the quality". In the study of Diaomu, the most important is to review the carving technique, and discuss the details later.

Authentication of Diaomu usually starts with the following:

Ⅰ. Identifying the texture. Diaomu is usually made from the most refined copper, thus there can not be sand holes. The copper should be glowing like gold, certainly there are exceptions.

Ⅱ. Examining the crafts. Diaomu is carved with knives or other tools, therefore, each streak on the coin is obvious, and the characters are certainly dainty, powerful and spirited. Under an amplifier, cut marks can normally be seen and the writing style is animated. There has been no chance for copper flowing or missing mold to happen to Diaomu.

Ⅲ. Weight. Diaomu must be bigger, heavier and thicker than the mother or sample coins molded after it. It feels heavy and substantial when holding Diaomu in the hand.

Ⅳ. Observing the color. Diaomu are few that are covered with patina. It is made from refined copper, which is golden and has an archaic tinge. The so-called black-paint-ancient and mercury-ancient in ancient coins are almost never seen in Diaomu. Some Diaomu looks shiny like a mirror, which is probably because the raw copper was polished before a Diaomu was made from it.

Other methods like listening and smelling (there should be no acid smell) and rubbing from inscription (there should be spirit) are used in authentication of Diaomu.

度量衡

收藏或研究中国古钱，我们一定要认识中国度量衡的演变。中国每一个朝代都有其尺寸的长短或斤两的轻重，值得我们注意的是，汉建初尺等于四个货泉的长度，唐尺等于十开元钱，而清排钱尺大概等于机制广东局光绪通宝十五枚。

所以从春秋末期到清代两千多年中，每尺的长度由 23 厘米左右增到 33.3 厘米，增大了 40% 之多。

至于重量方面，重量亦由每斤 250 克左右，增加到 600 多克。西汉五铢大概每枚是 3.5 克，如果每两是二十四铢，汉一两便是 16.8 克。由唐代直到清末，每钱是 3.73 克，所以库平一两是 37.3 克。（注：每市两是 31.25 克）

METROLOGY

It is necessary to know about the changes in Chinese metrology in collection or research of ancient Chinese money. There was length in chi and cun and net weight in jin and liang during each ancient Chinese dynasty. Of note is that a Jianchu chi in Han Dynasty equaled the length of four Huoquan, a Tang chi was the same as ten Kaiyuan money, and a paiqian chi in Qing Dynasty was largely fifteen GuangXu Tongbao made by Guangdong authority for making money.

Therefore, during over two thousand years from the late years of Spring and Autumn Period to Qing Dynasty, length of a chi changed from about 23 cm to 33.3 cm, with more than 40% increase.

As regard to weight, it also increased from about 250 g per jin to more than 600 g. A wuzhu of West Han Dynasty was approximately 3.5 g, so if one liang was 24 zhu, one liang of Han Dynasty would be 16.8 g. From Tang Dynasty all the way to Qing Dynasty, a qian was 3.73 g, so a kuping liang was 37.3 g. (Note: a liang is 31.25 g)

收集古钱的原则

我收集古钱已有数十年，为什么要收集古钱呢？当然是因为兴趣。

收集古钱与收集古玩一样，时人对古物的收藏，大多都为投资与保值。另一方面，收集古物可以了解当时的经济、政治、文化和科技等，尤其是与社会、文化和科技等有着密切的关系。

在某一个历史时期，其兵器的制造代表其科技的发展高度；而钱币的铸造，亦如此。因为钱币合金和铸造讲求速度，又要成本便宜，而且要防止伪造，没有一定的科技内涵是不成的。

铸钱除科技外，在一个动荡的社会，随着通货膨胀，货币面值增加，钱币面值改变，钱币在设计上亦有所变更。例如西汉王莽时期，有一刀平五千，又有六泉十布等小面值的辅币配合流通。这个时期最重要的是用阳范母去铸钱，完善了单范母迭铸钱的方法。

到了北宋时期，钱币又迎来了新的纪元。第一是用钱母铸钱，第二是大量铸造铁钱，第三是用胆水浸铜法来提炼铜铸钱。

到了元朝末期，兵乱，经济动荡，出现了历史上最大直径的流通钱。

在明朝后期，铸钱的金属由前朝的青铜（铜、锡和铅合金）改成使用黄铜（铜和锌合金），即明朝开始使用黄铜钱币。

清朝时期，着重用翻砂和雕母铸钱，清代雕母的雕刻技艺，成为历史上雕刻雕母之冠。

目前，文献所载的雕母数目不超过数百枚。本人喜欢收藏雕母，第一是数目稀少，第二是艺术性高，第三是不像其他古钱大量出土。我花了四十年的寻找，亦不过搜集到一百多枚，这些珍贵的雕母是这本书的核心。

PRINCIPLES FOR COLLECTING ANCIENT COINS

I have been collecting ancient coins for decades, but why ? Certainly it is about interest.

Just like collecting antiques, most people today collect ancient things for investment and maintenance of value. On the other hand, collecting ancient things can help understand economics, politics, culture and technology of that particular time, especially collecting coins, which are closely related to society, culture and technology, etc.

In some historical period, manufacturing of weapons represents the peak of its technology, whereas casting of coins also, reflects the level of its technology. Technology of a certain level is necessary to guarantee quickness in alloying and casting coins, to control the cost and to prevent forgery.

Apart from technology, the design will also change in a turbulent society due to inflation, increase in currency denomination and changes in the nominal value of money. Just like under Wang Mang's reign in West Han Dynasty, there were "Yidaopingwuqian", "Liuquanshibu" and so on, and the most important is that "Yangfanmu" was used to cast coins, perfecting the method of casting coins with single "Fanmu" overlying each other.

Coins entered a new epoch during North Song Dynasty because of, first, casting coins with "Qianmu"; second, casting a great amount of iron coins; third, extracting copper by immersing it in salt water to cast coins.

At the end of Yuan Dynasty, the war was going on with all its stresses and strains resulting in economic turmoil. The currency with the largest diameter (large round

Zhizheng coins）came into existence in history.

During later Ming Dynasty, the metals used for casting coins were changed from bronze （alloy of copper, tin and lead）to brass （alloy of copper and zinc）.

Fansha and Diaomu were mostly used to cast coins in Qing Dynasty. Diaomu of Qing Dynasty has become the King of Diaomu in history in terms of carving.

There are only several hundred of Diaomu recorded in literature up to now. I am interested in collecting Diaomu for several reasons: it is small in number, has high artistic quality and rather slim chance to be unearthed, unlike other ancient coins. I have spent 40 years searching for it and got only a little bit more than a hundred. These precious Diaomu are the core of this book.

落难的两枚雕母

我收藏古钱已有四十多年，研究雕母亦已有三十多年。我在《中国钱币》1998 年第三期发表了《雕母的讨论》后，因公事繁忙，没有空闲再去写述古钱。

不觉又十多年了，这些年间只在访香港时认识了关汉亨先生，关前辈对清代雕母钱研究有素，吾仰慕之至。后来在网上又认识了少泉（河北石家庄人），年纪小小，但对雕母的认识，在我之上，可惜我在美国，他们在中国香港和中国内地，见面的机会极少。

最近看到龚伟先生所写的《雕母祖钱鉴赏》一书，市面上说它是"世界第一部雕母祖钱专著"。内容不错，作者花了许多心思，但他所列的三十八品雕母祖钱，没有见过原物，我只能说见人见智。

集钱，以搜集雕母为最不易，有些收藏家终生不过。在上海博物馆里，数位古泉泰斗的藏品，亦不过数十枚而已。这三十多年来，我专心收藏清朝雕母，无论拍卖在中国、新加坡、日本、澳洲还是美国，或是中国香港、中国台湾等地区我都热心关注和投标，无论是小平、当五、当十、当五十、当百、当五百和当千等悉数购入。

以下两枚雕母，已开金口，流落民间，受尽风雨，一枚更是遍体鳞伤，令人可悲。图 38 为咸丰宝泉当五百，直径 5.65 厘米，重 64.9 克，应该是咸丰大钱初期的雕刻品，与马定祥主编的《咸丰泉汇》（第 263 页，1–7–20 小元）相似，可惜整体伤痕，之前拍卖时，无人问津，落标。十年前，由华辰辗转入了我的私箧中。

有人说，收集古钱，要收品相好的。可我认为，收集雕母，不论品相，只要是真品，就应该收集。雕母真是凤毛麟角之品，难遇亦难求。幸运的是，近年在古钱拍卖中偶有一两品，可惜都是雕母钱中的普通品，但亦是难得之品。

图 39 是咸丰宝源当百雕母，直径有 4.95 厘米，重 45.7 克，与《咸丰泉汇》（第 290 页，2–6–9 大当）一品相似，应该是咸丰大钱初中期之雕品。收购之时，转让者以为是母钱，但实际上是雕母，宝源雕母比宝泉雕母更难得，这枚雕母虽然已流通过，但手执这枚雕母时，仍爱不惜手，真有"人在钱中，钱在人中"之感。

图38

图39

以上两枚雕母，公诸于世，让能者去断定其真伪吧！

咸丰当十雕母（小型）

二十年前寻找母钱，一位日裔美国人找到这枚钱（图40），他说是母钱，当时叫价一千美元，我亦没有回价，看这枚钱品相好，就当它是母钱吧！隔了二十多年再拿出来看，欣喜若狂，手都颤抖了，原来这是枚雕母。图41是本雕母与其他普通（同样）钱比较。

图40　雕母——咸丰宝源当十

咸丰宝源雕母，直径为3.2厘米，重13.5克，厚0.3厘米。

咸丰宝源局·当十　盍宝八月

直径3.2厘米

雕母

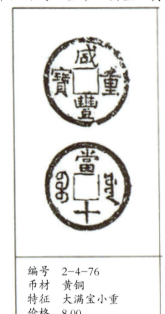

编号	2-4-76
币材	黄铜
特征	大满宝小重
价格	8.00

咸丰泉汇

直径3.0厘米

1788，咸丰重宝（背）宝源
（满文）当十　12.8克

上海博物馆

图41　雕母和其他普通（同样）钱比较

在未讨论这枚雕母以前，我们先引述《咸丰钱汇》中有关宝泉局和宝源局对咸丰当十的记载：

【宝泉局】

"咸丰年间，在太平天国革命打击下，清政府财政极端困难，遂行大钱。《光绪顺天府志》载：'咸丰三年，军旅数起，饷需支拙，东南道路梗阻，滇铜不至，刑部尚书周祖培，大理寺卿恒春，御史蔡绍洛先后条陈钱法，请改铸大钱，以充度支。下其议于户部，时寿阳祁隽藻权尚书，力赞成之。五月，先铸当十钱一种，文曰咸丰重宝，重六钱，与制钱相辅而行。'"

《东华录》："（咸丰）五年十月，'现值度支匮乏，军饷浩繁，开源节流，两无善策。自推行钞法添置大钱以来，京城官号所存宝钞及户、工两局铁钱局所铸当十、当五大钱均已日见流通，藉资周转。'这是因为零用钱不足，故铁钱开始时尚可流通始用。后大钱贬值，铁钱更为贬值。咸丰七年正月，市间已渐不行使铁钱，终于在咸丰九年七月，依绵愉等奏，铁钱局及户工铁钱炉座，一并裁撤。"

【宝源局】

"咸丰年间，因太平军兴，滇铜不达，宝源局与宝泉局一起，率先开始鼓铸大钱。据咸丰三年（1853年）九月二十五日户部尚书孙瑞珍、工部尚书翁心存会折中提到：'工部钱法衙门查宝源局前月铸制钱五卯，当十大钱一卯，今拟自十月起，留铸一钱重制钱二卯。'咸丰七年八月二十一日工部尚书许乃普在报告宝源局铸钱情况中提到：'本年入春以来，当五大钱日行壅滞，三月以后，街市概不行使。臣等公同商酌，已将当五钱一项，饬令暂行停铸，统铸当十钱十大卯。'"

从上文我们可以知道，咸丰三年（1853年）五月二十七日，户部开铸当十大钱，而工部亦大概在户部之后开铸当十，因在八月二十八日户部开铸当五十大钱，所以工部（保源局）铸当十应在六七月之间。

由于大钱在推行中到处碰壁，民间对大钱的抵制愈演愈烈，尤其是私铸四起，铜的来源越艰，减重越着，起初一枚当十在二十克左右，后来减到只有十克，宝泉局有的只在四克左右，重量和小平差不多。所以清政府不得不采取措施，咸丰五年（1855年），停铸当百当五十大钱，只铸当十钱。到了咸丰七年正月，当十大钱两吊抵钱一吊，咸丰八年（1858年）正月，当十钱只能当二、当三行使。咸丰九年（1859年）四月，当十钱只能当一行使了。所以铸造大钱不再有利，清政府只好停铸。从以上我们可以看到当十的铸造有四五年之久，而其他大钱，铸造时间不满一二年。关于当十钱的铸造，宝泉局最多，大概等于宝源的二三倍。

我在《中国钱币》（1998年第三期）已讨论过如何鉴定雕母钱，以后亦在各雕母钱稀品中，发表过各种鉴定雕母钱的方法。那么图40的雕母钱，除了用以前讨论过的各种方法鉴定外，我们这次从侧面观看这枚雕母（图42至图46）。图42是此雕母的正面侧看，图43是放大的"咸"字，左边是"咸"正本体，右边红的线条代表此钱边沿儿角度清晰，通常要手工雕刻出来才可以这样，不是雕母钱是很难有这样的雕刻的。

图42

图43

图44

图45

图46

同样看这枚雕母背面的侧面（图44），图45的红划是十字角划的清晰，而图46的红划是满文宝

源局的"源"字，这些字划和转角的雕工非常玲珑和巧妙，以上的论述是我们确定是不是雕母钱的一个关键。

在我的藏品中，还有数枚大型咸丰当十雕母，图47的宝源雕母，1984年得自 Money Company（美国加州洛杉矶县）；图48是宝泉当十，1993年得自北京旧识。

图47

图48

　　雕母难寻，懂鉴别的专家亦少，综上所述，希望年轻一辈的藏家能多看、多研究。现在每年在各拍卖行已有雕母钱拍卖，藏家在网上可以很容易找到真品收藏或相关照片来观看和研究。收藏是累积起来的，所以欲速则不达。

咸丰当五雕母

我花了四十多年时间寻找和收藏雕母钱，其中所花的时间和经受的辛苦是无法用语言描述的。

收藏中国古钱可以明白中国的历史和文化，历朝的兴衰，政治的动荡，铸造的技术等。通常社会不安、通货膨胀，古钱就会有别出的花样，如王莽的五泉十布，咸丰的当百当千圆钱。古钱又可以体现各朝代的科技水平，如明以前用青铜铸钱，明后期和清朝就多用黄铜翻砂技术制钱。

我的藏品中有一枚户部宝泉局当五雕母（图49、图51）和数枚工部宝源局雕母，图50和图52是其中之一枚。据《古钱大辞典》道："'户部宝泉局……，咸丰三年题准鼓铸当五'，而工部宝源局亦在咸丰三年题准鼓铸当五。"又说宝源局："当五，有许多种，铁钱未见。"而宝泉局《东华录》说："三年五月，辛末，始铸当十大钱荒。"所以当五应铸于五月之前。

图49和图51中的宝泉当五直径为2.9厘米，厚1.13厘米，而重为13.3克。图50和图52中的宝源当五直径为3.1厘米，厚1.04厘米，重为14.75克。

图49　咸丰宝泉当五雕母

图50　咸丰宝源当五雕母

图51　咸丰宝泉拓本（当五）

图52　咸丰宝源拓本（当五）

综上可见，当五钱存世量很少，在《马氏咸丰泉汇》中只记载了四枚宝泉局当五，而只有一枚雕母（图53），而宝源局有当五钱六十五枚，其中有雕母三枚，还有铁和铅钱。听说上海博物馆存有宝泉当五一枚，宝源当五钱十多枚。据考证，现在发现大概有十三个钱局在咸丰年间铸当五钱，咸丰宝泉局除当五（图54）尔宝外，其他的都是缶宝当五，种类又有八贝（貝）、离足贝（貝）和厶贝（貝）等。而宝源局当五钱大小不一，又只有尔宝，而"贝"字有八贝（貝）和离足贝（貝），更有厶贝（貝）和出头厶贝（貝），所以种类繁多。

马定祥先生认为："总的来说，咸丰宝源局的版别、数量不及宝泉局，唯宝泉当五因系试铸品，存世极少，而宝源当五系行用钱，故版别和数量均多。"

咸丰宝泉局·当五　缶宝八贝

壹	贰	壹	贰
编号 1-2-9 币材 黄铜 特征 祖价圆穿开口宝 价格 ★★★	编号 1-2-10 币材 黄铜 特征 开口宝 价格 ★★★	编号 1-2-11 币材 黄铜 特征 母钱开口宝 价格 ★★★	编号 1-2-12 币材 黄铜 特征 开口宝 价格 ★★★

图53　咸丰宝泉局（咸丰泉汇）

咸丰重宝（背）宝泉（满文）当五 6.8克

图54 戴书当五（上海博物馆）

清朝有规定：户部宝泉局铸钱充作军饷，工部宝源局铸钱备工程之需。同时还规定宝源局铸钱用于工部所管的各项工程，宝泉局铸钱供官民流通使用。

由此可见，宝泉局铸钱用于官民，所以宝泉局铸钱应多于宝源局。从马定祥先生的《咸丰钱汇》中可见，宝泉有875品，而宝源只有370品，小平宝泉有272品，而宝源只有80品，当十宝泉有320品，而宝源亦只有93品，比例大概三比一。但在泉汇中，当五就不同，比例是相反的。

图49宝泉当五没有图50宝源当五雕工好，文字亦没有宝源那么漂亮，而通常宝泉雕母比宝源雕母美，这是什么原因呢？我们有以下的解释：

1. 像马定祥先生所说，宝泉当五是试铸品。

2. 咸丰三年（1853年）初，军务紧急，滇铜不能继，在草速中铸宝泉当五钱。

3. 清入关后，首次铸大钱，所以比较草率，没有经过计划便铸钱。

4. 东华录："三年五月，辛未，始铸当十大钱"，传世的宝泉当十雕母刻于当五之后，并且都是精工细作。

5. 我搜集的这枚雕母和《咸丰泉汇》中（1-2-9）刻字的书法一样，它们都是不工整的，不同的是我的这枚已开金口。

6. 起初我认为图49雕母是母钱，但经过十多年的学习和研究，最终确定它是一枚雕母。起初是因为这枚雕母已经像其他钱一样在市面流通过，所以地章（肉）找不到明显的刀痕，但因此钱字划明显，没有砂眼，铜色美丽，钱体厚重等，最终确认为是一枚稀品。

7. 上海博物馆馆藏宝源局钱币中，普通品最重为8.7克，直径最大为2.9厘米。我收藏的雕母重量是14.75克，直径是3.1厘米。

8. 我收藏的宝源局雕母藏品直径是2.9厘米，和马定祥先生在《咸丰泉汇》书中所讲的雕母品直径相同，其重量是13.3克。上海博物馆馆藏的普通品是2.8厘米，而重量只有8.8克（图55）

咸丰重宝（背）宝源（满文）当五　8.3克

咸丰重宝（背）宝泉（满文）当五　8.8克　李伟先捐

图55　咸丰当五（宝泉宝源）（上海博物馆）

　　在结束这篇文章之前，我来说说寻找这枚雕母的奇遇吧。我在2001年到上海投资开办中美合资的上海东方国际医院，当时去拜访上海有名的藏家。由朋友引见郭若愚先生，由他处认识了华辰拍卖公司，经华辰公司负责人的关系，从私人藏家处得到图49的宝泉雕母，当时要价人民币五万元，我毫不犹疑地到银行取出五万元现金，买到了这枚雕母，想起来是一种缘分，当时还认为价格太贵，现在想来，是多么的幸运能找到这枚稀品。综上所述，收藏古钱是一门学问，要多看、多听、多寻找和多研究，一分耕耘，一分收获吧！希望同仁指教。

稀罕的宝蓟当百雕母

中国古钱币，历史悠久，形制特殊，先有刀布，后有方孔钱——有天圆地方之意。古代圆钱，先用青铜，到明中后期才有黄铜。初期用范铸法铸造钱币，后来用祖钱母钱，翻砂铸钱。起初钱币上以钱文纪重为主，如半两五铢，后来钱体上标注了朝代，如清朝的乾隆通宝、咸丰通宝。中国方孔钱有多种特征，与外国不同，古代钱币以铜为主，差不多不用金和银。中国书法艺术，体现于古钱中，还有许多古钱，用体积的大小或背文纪值来代表钱的面值。

中国方孔钱因为数量和品种很多，给收藏者以很大的收藏空间。各人可按自己所好，专心收藏和研究，也许可以成为某种钱币的专家。由于古钱是用溶铜合金所铸，所以每一枚铜钱都有它的特色。如每枚古钱的色泽、重量、铜绿、砂眼和流铜都不一样，故此坊间的书籍，只能作为参考，每枚钱币的真伪要靠收藏者多看、多收藏和同好切磋研究，才能有本事对每枚古泉的真假做确定。

我收集古钱已有四十多年，认识的前辈亦很多，我最仰慕的两位前辈是上海的马定祥先生和中国台湾的蔡养吾先生。虽然他们两位已离世，但与他们的友情是亘古不变的，这篇文章，是我写给他们的。我对中国古代面值大的古泉特别有兴趣，如元代的"至正通宝"和清代的"咸丰大钱"，特别是咸丰的雕母钱。

面值大的钱币通常出现于一个政治经济动荡的社会，如咸丰时期，发生太平天国起义，国库空虚，通货膨胀，金属短缺，铸造制钱已难进行，铸造面值大的钱币既可省金属原料，又可以省人工和时间，而面值又可以增大到当百当千，这样便可以应对金融短期的需求。从中国历史上来看，一个经济不稳定的社会，亦是一个钱制和形制改变和创新最为突出的时期，如王莽的五泉十布，元末至正通宝背吉权钞钱和咸丰各局的大面值的钱，如此更引起人们对大面值钱币收集的兴趣。

有人说大钱的特色：

1. 用料优良；

2. 铸造精美；

3. 质量出类拔萃；

4. 书法优秀；

5. 厚重超常；

6. 钱文别致。

我本人认为，面值大的钱币通常流通时间不长，磨擦损耗比小平钱少，在真伪方面判断比较容易。

又有人说咸丰大钱，版本极多而繁杂，如：

1. 币值复杂；

2. 重量变化大；

3. 钱名复杂；

4. 材料——各种不同金属或合金；

5. 文字复杂。

我自从一九九八年发表《雕母讨论》一文后，因公务繁忙，匿迹泉坛已十多年，数年前在香港和关汉亨先生会面一次，瞬眼间，我已七十多岁高龄。数十年来我专意收藏清代雕母，希望将来能一一公诸于世。

宝蓟局，是清代直隶蓟州（今天津蓟县）的铸局，立于清顺治二年（1645 年），废于雍正年间，至咸丰四年（1854 年）重启，停废时间长达一百三十多年。

咸丰四年（1854 年），因军事需要，宝蓟局重开，马兰镇总兵庆锡在奏文中提到"于开七月中旬开炉试铸"，因停废时间太久，炉座人员皆需重新配备和培训，又因改轻铸钱分量，私铸成风，加上原料缺乏，面值大，铸工粗糙，所以庆锡的奏文中说："当百大，钱一万九千余个，私铸约有六七成之多。"所以有"外来商人罢市，兵丁不愿用"，导致推行难，于同年十二月停铸，所以实际铸造时间应该只有几个月。

据马定祥先生的《咸丰钱汇》中说，宝蓟局曾铸小平、当五、当十、当五十和当百等五种钱，其书中收录 27 枚钱，其中只有小平一枚，当百三枚。所以理论上，宝蓟局从咸丰四年以后已不铸钱，在同治和光绪年间，不可能有宝蓟局的钱出现。

在蔡养吾先生所著的《中国古钱讲话》一书中，对咸丰宝蓟局当百铜钱的统计，平均重量为 54.4 克，如果超过这个重量的当百钱，应该是赝品或中央所铸颁发到地方的样钱。

宝蓟当百雕母，图 56 是笔者所藏的一枚宝蓟当百雕母，直径是 5.45 厘米，重量是 89.7 克，其形制与马先生收集的咸丰宝蓟局当百（编号 4-5-1）相同。

图56　宝蓟当百雕母

这枚雕母铜质上乘，字体清秀，有铁划银勾之感。每一勾一划一撇和一点，看来有一气呵成之感，雕工之精美是现代机器做不出的。用放大镜看，隐约可见到刀迹，看"咸"字的"口"，"宝"字的"目"，"丰"字的上半部，"当"字的"田"，"百"字"日"等的内部凹凸处，不但工整，而且条纹亦有一定的规则。最后，鉴别雕母的真伪，最重要的是，真正的雕母是不会有流铜和砂眼出现于钱的任何部位。注意，有时因为工匠不小心留下了一些没有磨掉的铜屑碎，这些是尖细的屑碎，和圆滑的流铜是有区别的。

图57

背吉大钱、满文宝蓟和宝吉，中国古代的背吉大钱以至正之宝权钞（背吉）为最（图58）。到了清光绪十年（1884年）吉林省铸吉字圆孔银币（图59），以后光绪、宣统两朝的银铜币，有单字汉文"吉"字或单字满文"吉"字的样本。

图58 至正之宝权钞（作者本人藏品）

图59 吉林省铸吉字圆孔银币

光绪宝吉制钱，据说始于1887年，炉址设在吉林临江门一带，由商捐官办，六月开铸，旧时本地人叫它为麻钱，以小平为主（图60），1889年更用机制钱（图61），到1908年归吉林银图局，停铸制钱。

正面　　　　　　　　　　反面

图60　光绪宝吉制钱

图61　机制钱

从图56咸丰当百宝蓟的满文"ᢒ"和图60至图61的满文"ᢒ"，两者的满文相同，传满文没有音韵，所以蓟和吉都是同音，写法完全一样。有趣的是，光绪通宝套子钱，其中蓟的"ᢒ"满文的写法则不同（图62），但光绪套子钱是臆造钱，一套二十个，应不是出于宝蓟局，因为宝蓟局在咸丰四年（1854年）以后已不存在。咸丰及以前的古钱，读"蓟"，光绪和宣统时期应读"吉"。望海内外泉友指正。

图62 光绪套子钱

两枚清宝黔雕母

收藏古泉易，收集精品就不易了。寻找清雕母难，除工、户两局，寻找其他局的更难。近来，有人投稿，也有人在网上，更有人著书说他们有稀世之雕母，虽都是长篇大论，可惜大部分都是空谈。

马定祥先生对宝黔局有这样的一段论述："据《制钱通考》记载，'康熙六年（1667年）户部题准复开各省炉座并添设铸局，……贵州背铸贵字，康熙九年停止。'但至今未发现康熙通宝背贵字钱。"由此可见，我们只能说宝黔局制钱是始于雍正年间。宝黔局是清代的铸币机构，雍正八年（1730年）在毕节县第一次开炉，在贵州前后有三个制钱的地方，第一是毕节县，乾隆二十四年（1759年）尾停，第二是在贵阳府，第三是在大定府，乾隆三十五年（1770年）开炉。

黄雅迪所写的《清代宝黔局历朝初铸部颁行用钱研究》和解飞所写的《宝黔局略论》对宝黔局铸钱的研究很有心得。黄雅迪对宝黔背当五十大钱有下面的叙述："当五十类铸币由于史料缺乏及宝物缺乏，马定祥先生在《咸丰钱汇》中引用耿宗仁先生拓片，定该钱为'祖钱部颁式'，铸币实物未见传世，应为试铸性质。近年有泉友披露于贵州安顺发现宝黔当五十铅质钱币，虽风格尚好，但因实物未见，仅凭图片难断其真伪。"黄雅迪又对同治重宝宝黔当十，有下面的解析："当十类铸币行用品未见，应为早期试铸性质，未正式铸造。"

马定详先生在《咸丰泉汇》书中有以下的记载："除小平钱外，宝黔局还有当十、当五十大钱。关于咸丰大钱的铸造情况，在咸丰三年（1853年）十一月初七日贵州巡抚蒋霨远的奏文中提到：'宝黔局改铸大钱，试行使用。'奏文中还提到：'铸钱工本每银一两仅可铸钱一千一百九十文，现市价二千文至二千一二百文，本省百文以上交易多用银，交通不便，搭放兵饷亦不易。办大钱，事属创举，不易适行。'今见宝黔局当十钱，黄铜质，依部颁样钱式铸造。……当五十大钱，《中国近代货币史数据》之'各局铸造咸丰大钱类别明细表'列有重宝'样钱'。《中国钱币》1983年第2期所载中国历史博物馆馆藏咸丰钱中，亦有宝黔当五十钱。但实物长期未见。蒙耿宗仁提供宝黔当五十部颁式样钱拓本，始一睹该钱之真面目。（图63）"

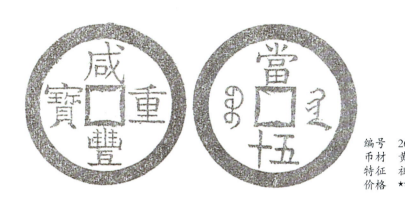

编号　26
币材　黄铜
特征　祖钱
价格　★★

图63　咸丰宝黔局·当五十

图64　宝黔　部颁　样钱

茫溪游鱼在网上发表《宝黔局咸丰当五十部颁样母钱发现始末》一文，颇有个人意见，可惜我们没有见到原物，所以不能给予任何评价。从网上和各类参考书籍，很容易找到宝黔局背当十和当五十样本，不过亦未见过原物，所以不能辨别它们的真伪。还有人说见过当五十铅钱，真假待考。

现在，我们认为马定祥先生的宝黔当五十（图63）和《简明钱币辞典》（上海古籍出版社）一书中的宝黔当十（图64）为真品。

宝黔局铸钱稀少，尤其是大钱，是由于下面的因素：

一、《故宫清钱谱》黄霄鹏编："……，宝黔俱未见大钱，由于太平天国战争，制钱部颁制度不能有效地管制或废除，而大钱铸期时间太短，所以五十大钱没有铸造或很少量的铸造。而当时钱为数亦不多。"

二、如上文马定祥老前辈引用贵州巡抚蒋霨远之奏文："……，本省百文以上交易多用银，交通不便，搭放兵饷亦不易。办大钱，事属创举，不易通行。"

三、宝黔局用铜六铅四配比，贵州铅锌产量丰富，但铜要采购于云南，清云南铜矿可以私营，贵州多铅锡，加上贵州地处边陲，山林密布，有冶炼铅锌和铸币的大量薪炭，加上贵州偏僻地多，官府查访和缉拿困难，所以私铸四起。罗时法在《清代贵州货币铸造的两个问题》中有说："贵州私铸的主要办法有三：一是利用当地丰富的铅锌，以铜一铅九为成色，配铸。二是销毁官钱，掺入铅沙。三是减重'重不过四分'。"

四、其他铸钱少的原因：

1. 贵州铅锌林木富饶，虽然偏僻，交通不便，但外省交易大，用银两比较方便，所以钱的需求减少；

2. 私铸和毁坏官钱滥，所以铸官钱成本太高，没有多铸钱的必要；

3. 贵州当时交通不便，铸钱人材缺乏，技术不高，所以铸钱劣而不美，不为民所爱，加上私铸祸盛，所以官铸钱大减。

在我的藏品中，有两枚宝黔雕母，一为同治背黔当十，另一枚为咸丰背黔当五十。

同治当十背黔（图65），此钱直径3.5厘米，重24.5克，它与图64宝黔局部颁样钱差不多，但满文"宝黔"是大样，未开金口铸钱，此钱是同治宝十稀有之品，亦是唯一知道的雕母。

咸丰当五十宝黔（图66），此钱直径5.6厘米，重60.8克，此枚雕母雕工精美，字划明晰，神气生猛，开门见山之品。起初我们以为和马老所说耿宗仁提供的一枚不同，但仔细研究，是拓本技术和拓墨不同，两枚拓本字划重迭无差，应是同一雕母，所以这枚钱是海内孤品。虽然我收藏这枚雕母多年，但直至最近才发现其庐山真面目，真是喜出望外。

图65

图66

以下做一些琐谈，可以助泉友辨别雕母的真假：

一、雕母的边

1. 宝黔五十是平边的，金口已开，钱有蜡似的痕迹，看来曾用此枚雕母铸过钱。（图 67）

2. 同治当十未开金口，边是弧或圆的（图 68），以前我们讨论过，这种尖圆的边可以翻砂铸钱树，铸成的钱树，钱与钱之间或钱与干之间可以分离。马老的《咸丰泉汇》书中有数枚母钱是未开金口的，其他文献亦有记载。

二、雕母的字划——直线

1. 图 69 是同治当十的"同"字，"同"字的右边垂划宽，其边所刻下的角度比较大，而在钱肉上看到很长的刀痕，刀痕是雕母的一种特色，当然刀痕可以随时伪造。

2. 图 70 是宝黔五十的"宝"字，字内的"贝"横划细幼，这种横划所刻下的角度比较狭，再看划与划之间的口形，其底部很幼而狭。

三、雕母的口大细

图 71 的宝黔五十的"重"字，中间田字的四个口大，所以这种大的口，其内部会呈四方或长方的（肉）平面。

四、金属屑（尖）

图 72 的宝黔当五十的"咸"字右边和图 73"当"字的右边口字上角都有长尖形的金属屑，这些呈尖形的金属屑是雕刻时留下的，这些屑是尖的，通常普通古钱铸造时留下的流铜（合金）是呈圆锥状而又是圆滑似的。除了刀痕之外，这种金属屑是鉴定雕母的另一种方法。

五、图 74 是宝黔"五十"两字和图 75 宝黔的"丰"字上半部，如果用蜡或墨来拓这些字样，一不小心，十的左边横划的尖端和丰字上部左边直划的上端是拓不出来的。这些明晰的尖端结构亦是一种辨认雕母真假的方法。

六、图 76 是宝黔五十划的"宝"字，看斜横划的下面，可以看到这些地方和钱肉面不是平坦的，这是雕刻时的一种技术问题，如果用机器雕刻，就会排除这些问题。

上面的论述，见人见智，望读者指教。

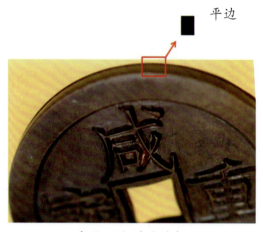

宝黔五十（平边）

图67

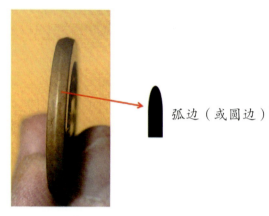

同治当十（圆边）

图68

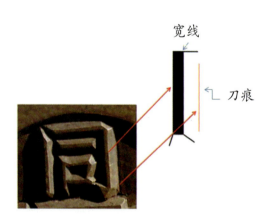

同治当十（宽线条）

图69

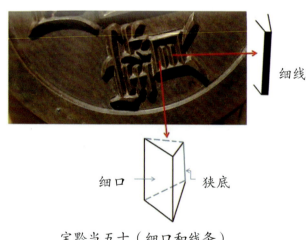

宝黔当五十（细口和线条）

图70

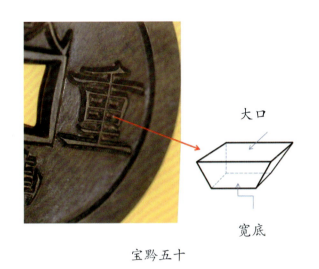

大口

宽底

宝黔五十

图71

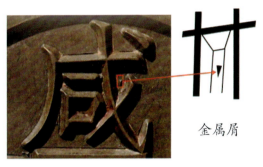

金属屑

宝黔五十（金属屑）

图72

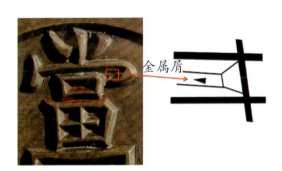

金属屑

宝黔五十（金属屑）

图73

不能拓的边
（字划）

能拓的边
（字划）

宝黔五十（拓本——普通技术）

图74

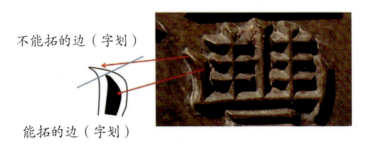

不能拓的边（字划）

能拓的边（字划）

宝黔五十（拓本——普通技术）

图75

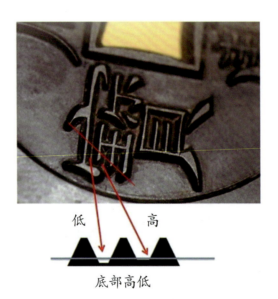

低　　　高

底部高低

宝黔五十（各种底部）

图76

一枚天下大平雕母钱

　　"天下大平"一词，见于汉镜背面的图案（图77），又见于坊间手工有四孔的"天下大平"和"文王百子"的银刻花钱上（图78）。目前，还见不到铸有"天下大平"花钱，常见的是铸有"天下太平"的花钱（图79）。

　　"天下太平"花钱或宫钱以清代为多。传世有清早期的满汉文"天下太平"钱（图80）。后来才多用面年号背天下的太平钱（图79），这种钱自乾隆至宣统均有，道光、咸丰最多，宣统罕见，所以有人说这些钱俗称为"太平钱"。

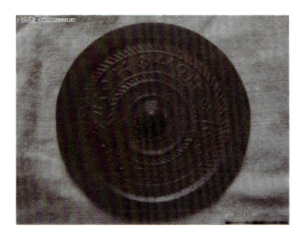

图77　天下大平铜镜面

图78　天下大平银刻花钱

图79　普通咸丰天下太平钱

图80　满汉文天下太平

私铸或私刻钱

图81（a）

图81（b）

私铸

图81（c）

这种钱在民间都有铸或手工刻造，而字样亦有异，图81（a）（b）（c），但我们所注重的是宫廷所用的。在传世中，我们可以见到"天下太平"的开炉钱树（图82）和葫芦钱（图83），图81（a）（b）是嘉庆道光背天下太平花钱。所以有人说清代的皇帝铸造"天下太平"吉语宫钱，是用于祭祀祈福、节日祝贺、坠灯、压帐、赏赐、上梁或作镇物等用途。这些太平钱，在铜质上和制作上都比一般普通钱讲究和美。

图82　开炉钱树

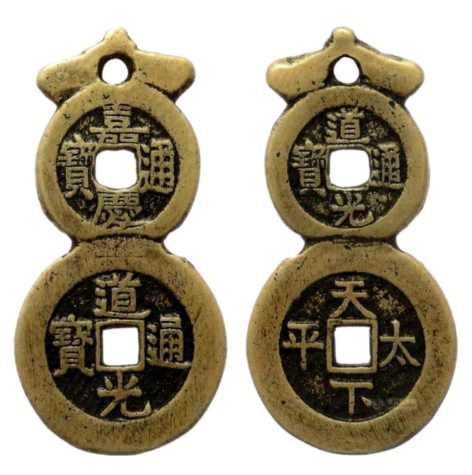

图83　葫芦钱（挂用）

　　现已知的"天下太平"雕母钱寥寥可数，正如图85的道光通宝，在"天下大平"雕母钱之前，在传世中有一种背"一统天下"的咸丰通宝（图86），又只有数个版本，所以有人认为面咸丰通宝，背"一统天下"和"天下太平"是对钱。

（a）

（b）

图84　嘉庆道光背天下太平钱

图85　道光天下太平雕母

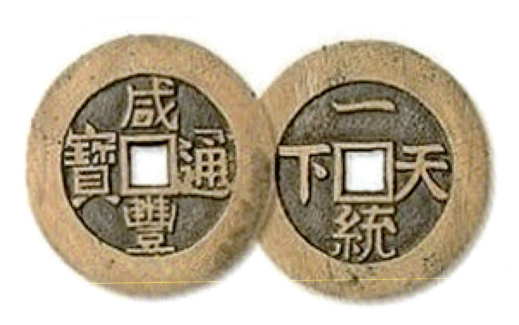

图86　咸丰背一统天下

图 87 是我收藏的"天下大平"的雕母钱，重 36.8 克，直径 4.6 厘米（图 88），雕工精美，肉平坦，其造型与道光、咸丰钱制作相似（图 89、图 90），所以应是铸于咸丰早期，因为咸丰后期的钱肉面通常凸起。咸丰时期，受太平天国之扰，内忧外患，所以王权希望天下太平，又因有太平天国之乱，或许是这样，才雕"天下大平"钱，所以要天下大平才可能有天下太平。这枚钱真是海内外孤品。

图87　咸丰天下大平雕母钱

图88　天下大平钱拓本

图89　道光天下太平钱

图90　咸丰背天下太平

　　在故宫博物馆有一枚金戒指，上面铸有"大清一统天下太平"（图91），和背一统天下的咸丰通宝（图86）都是咸丰后期铸造的。我的藏品中有一枚皇家之印，刻着"一统天下"（图92），图93是印款。从这些看来，当时清宫愿望"天下大平"。

图91　大清一统天下太平戒指

图92　一统天下玛瑙玉玺

图93　一统天下印款

高10厘米　方5.2厘米

这些雕母献给泉友欣赏，如今四海升平，正如有人说"张灯结彩嘉年华，天下太（大）平庆新春"。

思贤藏品

清代玉件

注：大概用于进呈雕母时用。

以下我的藏品有的来自拍卖行或古董商，有些得自各藏家和民国初年的军阀或前清的名门世家。

四十多年的收藏来之不易。

自古鉴定古钱，以六字真言为主，那就是"文、质、声、色、味、神"。

传闻民国初期前清工匠伪刻雕母，清后期已开始用机制钱，当时人的寿命很短，大概五十左右，所以到民国，工匠大部分都已年长，工艺好的，寥寥可数。所以我们认为当时雕刻的赝品，应只限于小平，大钱比较难雕刻，而且难以藏匿缺点。

雕母的真赝更要关注雕工、雕痕、锉痕、刀痕和钉印等。材料大部分是精铜，此外还有少数取材于木质和牙质等。

确定雕母的主要一点就是看肉，肉可以有纹，但不可以有砂眼。每字划旁大部分呈现刀纹。

至于内外廓，两者都能有 R 角或 C 角。R 圆角（RADIVS）是指内圆弧角或外圆弧角，而 C 倒角（CHAMFER）是指一般 45 度左右的倒角。

R 角　　　　　　　　　　C 角

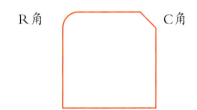

另外直角边缘（RIGHT ANGLE EDGE)，外廓只见于雕母，雕母内廓比较复杂，后面我再用图解析。

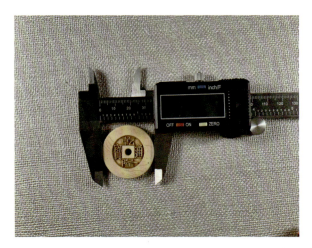
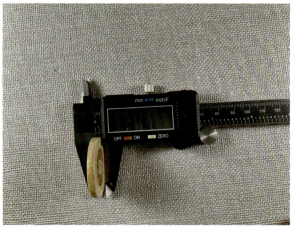

数码卡尺

测量本书样品重量和尺寸的工具

雕母印　　　　　　母钱印　　　　　　普通钱

雕母、母钱和流通钱的比较

	雕母	母钱	普通钱
直径	大	中	小
拓本字刻	幼	中	粗
肉	平滑	小砂眼	多砂眼
模印字刻	粗	幼	
通字田部	明显	不太明显	模糊

雕母、母钱和流通钱比较

雕母　　　　母钱　　　　流通钱

 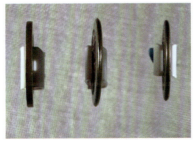

侧   上

外廓的 R 角或 C 角

注：通常雕母才有直角。

四方　　　　　　　　金口　　　　　　　　圆

嘉庆时期的雕母内廓孔和金口

四方孔
道光前期多四方孔

圆孔
道光后期多圆孔

金口开

清代雕母的穿孔

母范
每钱中都有点

内廓留下的点

画规的中点（王莽时期）

注：这个是画规留下来的点，从母范到子钱。

光绪时期留下画规痕的雕母

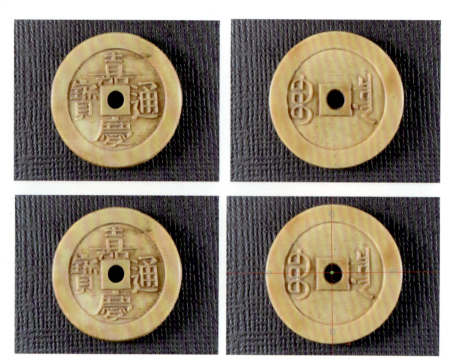

牙雕的点（一）

注：用外廓四点来决定钱的中点。

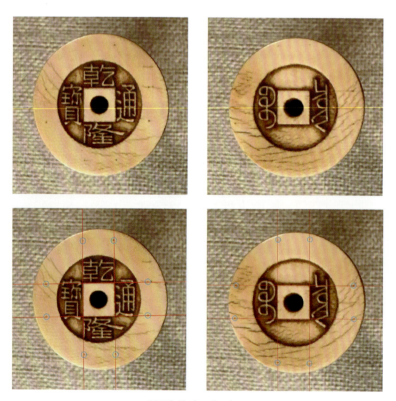

牙雕的点（二）

注：用外廓八点来决定内廓的位置等。

在雕母上留下的刀痕和锉痕（一）

在雕母上留下的刀痕和锉痕（二）

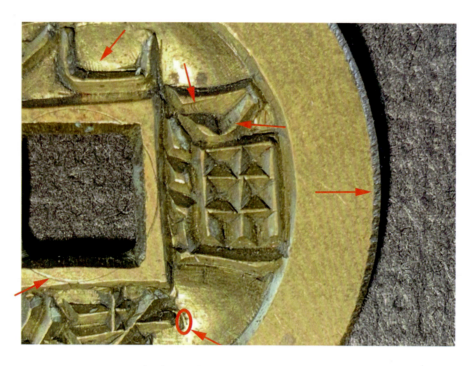

在雕母上留下的刀痕和锉痕（三）

正面影

内廓胶塑

斜面影曲度

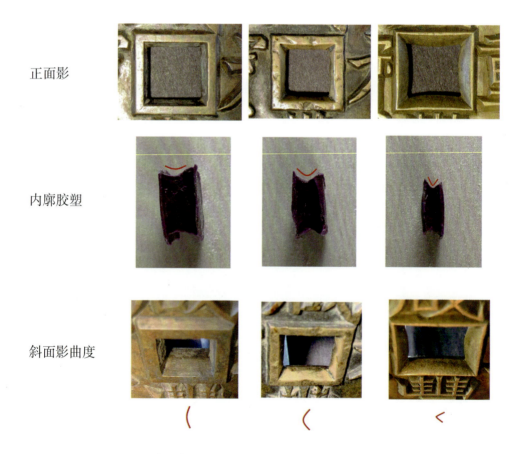

雕母内廓开金口的各种 R 角或 C 角

雕母 R 角的立体

鎏金钱

中国鎏金最少有二千年的历史。唐代开元钱鎏金用水银和金，清代鎏金有的先将铜钱镀银后才鎏金。

注：镀银就是将铜钱放在银水溶液内，起化学作用，铜钱面上就镀上一层银，和宋朝胆水浸铜法相似。这样鎏出来的金钱表面颜色像 24K 金。另外，可以用银汞膏，先镀银，再上金。

附录

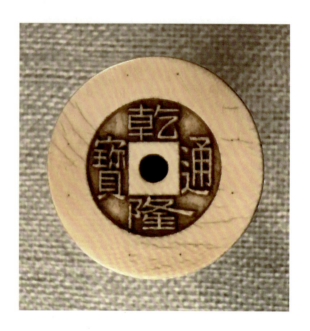

1. ★★★乾隆通宝背宝泉局

直径：34.6 毫米

厚度：4.3 毫米

重量：5.9 克

备注：牙雕。面和背都有八点
针孔。

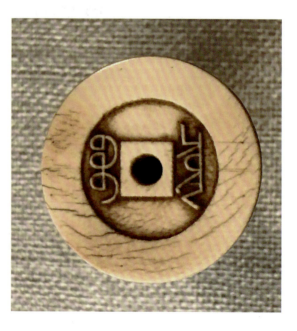

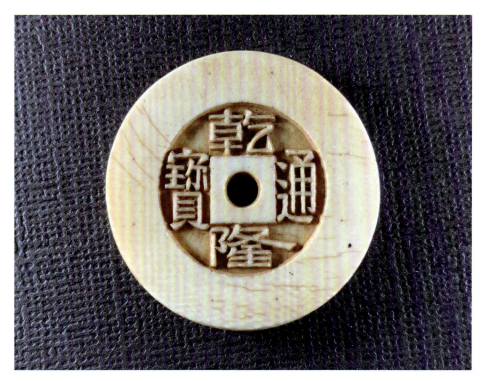

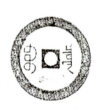

2. ★★嘉庆通宝背宝泉局

直径：27 毫米

厚度：2.2 毫米

重量：1.9 克

备注：牙雕。钱背有四点针或
其他利器孔痕。

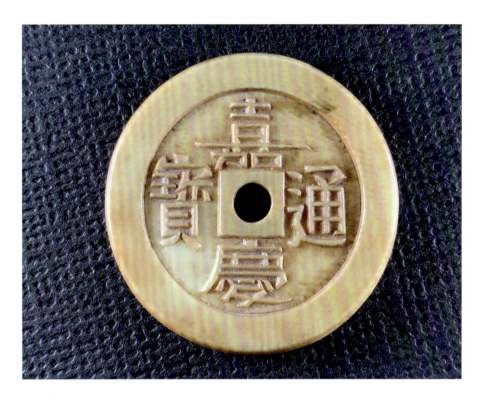

3. ★★★宣统通宝背宝泉局

直径：26毫米

厚度：1.9毫米

重量：1.4克

备注：郝凤亮老师对牙质有疑问，后确定为玳瑁。唐代有玳瑁开元钱。

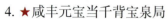

4. ★咸丰元宝当千背宝泉局

直径：62.9 毫米

厚度：4.6 毫米

重量：76.2 克

备注：华辰 2003 年北京拍卖所得。

应为样钱，参看马定祥《咸丰泉汇》

P230。

母或样钱——字和肉都有砂眼。

5. ★道光通宝背宝源局

直径：24.1 毫米

厚度：1.5 毫米

重量：4.2 克

备注：陈京元旧藏（母钱）。

此枚铜质带绿，似为失蜡法铸造，

边沿儿成尖圆，是母钱的风格。

母钱——肉砂眼，字划不清晰。

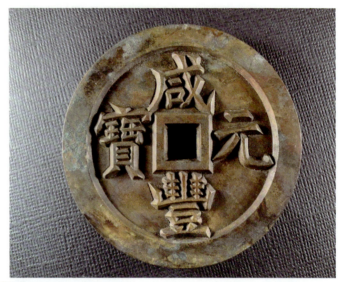

6. ★★★★★咸丰元宝当千背
宝泉局

　　直径：67.4 毫米

　　厚度：7.3 毫米

　　重量：171.8 克

　　备注：祖钱内廓大满宝。参看
《咸丰泉汇》当千缶宝八贝闭口宝。

雕母——肉平滑，字工整，字傍有痕，外阔工整。

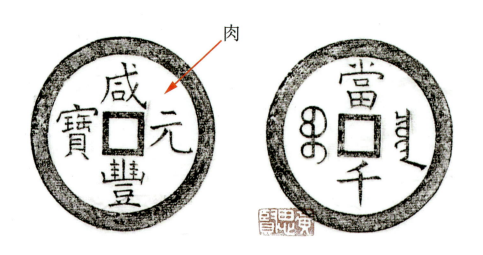

7. ★★★★★咸丰元宝当千背
宝源局

直径：62.8 毫米

厚度：5 毫米

重量：95.3 克

备注：参看《咸丰泉汇》咸丰
宝源局当千缶宝出头ス贝。

雕母——肉平滑，字旁有刀纹，铜质美，字秀丽。

肉无砂眼

8. ★★★★咸丰元宝当五百背
宝泉局

直径：58.4 毫米

厚度：4.3 毫米

重量：69.3 克

备注：华辰 2003 年北京拍卖
所得。雕母。参看《咸丰泉汇》
P163。

流通过雕母——肉平滑，字角尖而美，而拓本看不出来。

9. ★★★★咸丰元宝当百背
宝泉局

直径：54.8 毫米

厚度：4.8 毫米

重量：73 克

备注：参看《咸丰泉汇》
P141。此枚边沿儿是斜边。

清代雕母研究
Study on the Carved Pattern Coin of Qing Dynasty

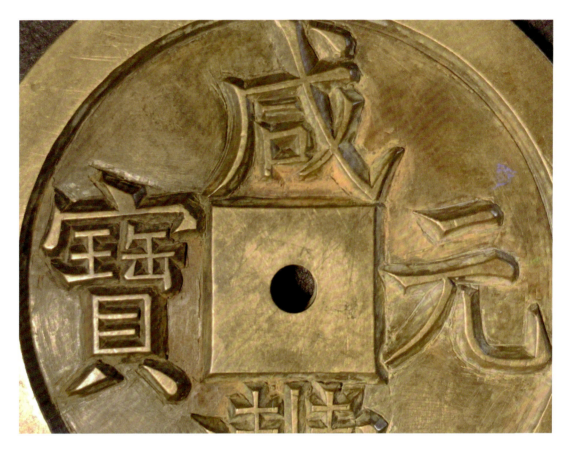

雕母——肉平无砂，刀痕，字娟秀。

10. ★★★★咸丰重宝当五十背
宝泉局

直径：44 毫米

厚度：4.8 毫米

重量：47.4 克

备注：参看《咸丰泉汇》P119。
此枚鎏金，但已几乎全褪落。

鎏金雕母——内平滑鎏金，字角尖似针。

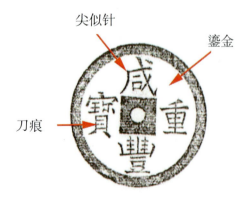

11. ★★★咸丰重宝当十背宝泉局

直径：33.7 毫米

厚度：2.3 毫米

重量：14.1 克

备注：此枚是美国 Money Co.1984
年在中国香港拍卖一个月后，在美国洛
杉矶总公司售出。

雕母——整体平滑，"重"中"車"字字划角度清晰。

12. ★★★咸丰重宝当十背宝
源局

直径：33 毫米

厚度：2.9 毫米

重量：13.5 克

备注：二十世纪九十年代美籍
日本人 Dennis Nakano 当时以为是
母钱，以1800美元成交。后确认
为雕母。

流通过雕母——肉面光滑，字秀美，"重"字尖端像尖刀。

字尖端像尖刀

字尖端像尖刀

字尖端像尖刀

13. ★★★★咸丰重宝当十背
宝泉局

　　直径：37.6 毫米

　　厚度：3.5 毫米

　　重量：26.3 克

　　备注：参看《咸丰泉汇》P89。

雕母——像其他雕母，"咸"口中角度分明。

斜角线条分明

刀痕

14. ★ ★ ★ 咸丰重宝当五背
宝源局

　　直径：31.7 毫米

　　厚度：2.7 毫米

　　重量：14.9 克

　　备注：参见《咸丰泉汇》
P248。

雕母——除其他雕母特征外，肉有各种刀纹。

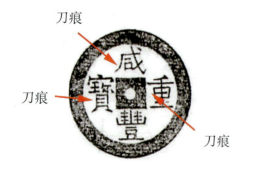

刀痕

刀痕

刀痕

15. ★★★ 同治重宝当十背
宝泉局

直径：32.6 毫米

厚度：2.8 毫米

重量：16.8 克

备注：金口开。

雕母——雕工不精，但处处有刀纹，肉有刀痕，但无砂眼。

16. ★★★同治重宝当十背宝
源局

　　直径：32.7 毫米

　　厚度：3.6 毫米

　　重量：21.5 克

　　备注：此雕母的边沿儿是斜的。

雕母——每字都有刀纹，肉无砂眼。

刀纹，肉无砂眼

刀纹，肉无砂眼

刀纹，肉无砂眼

刀纹，肉无砂眼

17. ★★★★同治重宝当十背宝福局

直径：34.6 毫米

厚度：3 毫米

重量：19.6 克

备注：十年前跟少泉先生通话，曾言从未见过同治宝泉和宝源外的当十雕母。这枚应为孤品，边沿儿亦是斜边。另有数枚其他地方局藏品，如宝黔、宝云等。

雕母——字工整，多刀痕。

刀痕

刀痕

刀痕

刀痕

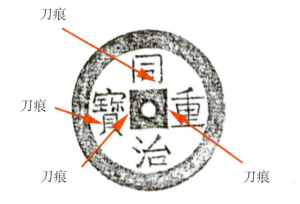

18. ★★★光绪重宝当十背宝泉局

直径：34 毫米

厚度：2.4 毫米

重量：15.6 克

备注：2002 年，在上海结识郭若愚前辈，他有数枚咸丰和光绪当十，可惜当时未拍照和制拓，其后这数枚雕母不知所踪。此枚与郭老藏品相似。

雕母——肉平滑而多刀纹，字划廋尖。

19. ★★★雍正通宝背宝浙局

直径：26.7 毫米

厚度：2 毫米

重量：8.45 克

备注：中圆孔。

雕母小平——字划深处角度分明，肉平滑但留下刀纹。

20. ★★★乾隆通宝背宝泉局

直径：27.5 毫米

厚度：1.8 毫米

重量：7.9 克

备注：乾隆雕母，中孔许多是
四方孔。

雕母小平——"通"内田字斜角划分明，无砂眼，有刀痕。

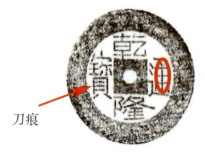

刀痕

田字斜角划分明

21. ★★★★嘉庆通宝背宝泉局

直径：26.4 毫米

厚度：1.3 毫米

重量：4.9 克

备注：背面鎏金，大部分尚存，很美。

小平雕母（鎏金）——"通"字字划分明，肉有刀痕。

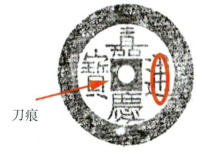

刀痕

"通"字字划分明

22. ★★★道光通宝背宝泉局

直径：26.4 毫米

厚度：1.7 毫米

重量：6.9 克

备注：圆孔。

小平雕母——字傍都有刀痕，内廓之间留下许多刀痕。

23. ★★★道光通宝背宝源局

直径：25.6 毫米

厚度：2.2 毫米

重量：7.4 克

备注：已故陈京元先生旧藏。
美国长堤拍卖（1991 年）。

流通过的雕母小平——历尽沧桑留下各种纹，字体工整。

字划旁留下的刀刻纹

字划旁留下的刀刻纹

字划旁留下的刀刻纹

字划旁留下的刀刻纹

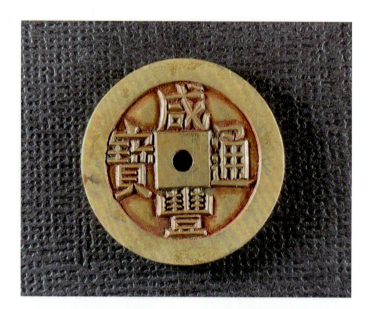

24. ★★★咸丰通宝背宝泉局

直径：24.9 毫米

厚度：2 毫米

重量：7.6 克

备注：开口贝。

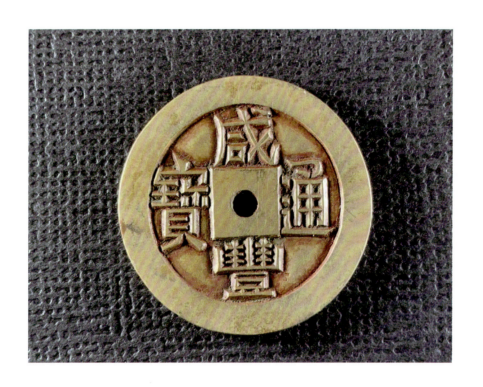

小平雕母——字尖如针。

25. ★★★咸丰通宝背宝源局

直径：26.3 毫米

厚度：1.9 毫米

重量：7.25 克

备注：闭口贝。

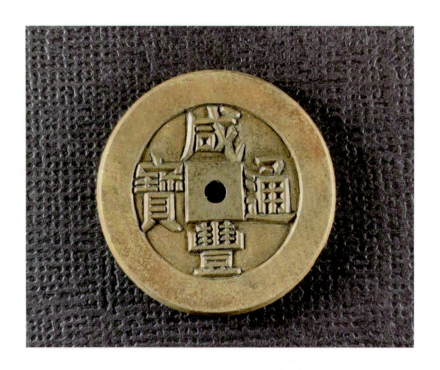

小平雕母——四处都有刀纹，"咸"的"口"部和"通"的"用"部 X–Y 线条明显。

26. ★★★ 同治通宝背宝泉局

直径：27.4 毫米

厚度：1.9 毫米

重量：8.2 克

备注：出头宝。

小平雕母——"通"字X部角度分明,"通"字下和其他地方多刀纹。

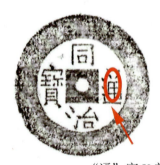 

"通"字X部角度分明

27. ★★光绪通宝背宝泉局

直径：24 毫米

厚度：1.8 毫米

重量：5.3 克

备注：钱面有圆规痕迹。此钱得
自 Scott Semans 先生处。

雕母——有画规纹和其他刀痕。

画规纹

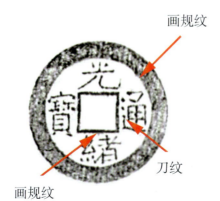

画规纹

刀纹

28. ★宣统通宝背宝泉局

直径：24.6 毫米

厚度：2.5 毫米

重量：8.6 克

备注：雕工劣。

雕母小平——遍体鳞伤的刀痕。

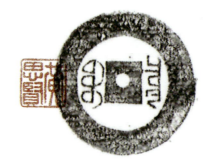

后记

清代雕母有据可查者近四百枚，归藏博物馆二百余枚，北京故宫博物院、上海博物馆略平分秋色，藏于民间者不足两百枚。

一年前，偶然从网上结识美籍华人黄思贤前辈，前辈学识渊博，精通医学，悬壶济世，年近耄耋。每以人生境遇、医学困惑不惧而上问，前辈则宅心仁厚，逢问必答，垂怜之极。愚乃区区鲁钝小辈，有此殊遇，无以为报。恰前辈十年前集成一本雕母研究专著，因公私繁忙，至今日方得闲出版。惟海外古泉研究者稀，意在两岸择地发行，嘱愚联系出版事宜，愚岂敢不效犬马尽心竭力？此为最初缘起。

然愚终为门外人，古泉尚无研究，何论雕母？后有幸结识郝凤亮前辈（网名东胡），将书稿请郝前辈指正，两位前辈似华山论剑，无刀光剑影却掀滔天波澜，让愚如痴如迷酣然若醉，慨世间难遇之奇事。后经黄前辈忙中偷闲劳心劳力拍照，更发未泯童心自研排图，又经郝前辈严格把关，多番努力，此书终面世。

黄老前辈集四十余年之功，藏清代雕母百余枚，恐海内外无人可及。海内外钱币同好、专家学者若能推敲研究文字、细品珍藏图鉴、体个中曲折故事，可听高山流水之音。

黄前辈之雕母的讨论文章、雕母和母钱对照的精微图片以及伪造雕母方法等数篇论述，阐雕母鉴定之核心，开藏识智慧之直路，乃千金难求之纸墨，切莫一瞥而过。

黄前辈鉴别雕母心得须辨材质、验雕工、称重量、观锈色。材质常为金黄色精铜，光亮如镜，几无铜锈。若材质现砂眼，则可判伪。黄前辈此次公布 28 枚雕母资料中现两枚牙雕质、一枚玳瑁质，均为罕见大珍品，又见两枚鎏金雕母，其时心情澎湃，观而忘食。

雕母乃用凿刻工具雕凿而成，字划清晰有神，放大可见刀痕，笔锋流畅自然，不可现流铜、错范。改刻、失蜡法伪品，多需用心琢磨，方不至落陷；仿刻品，细辨材质字体，亦可免入圈套。黄老前辈用心比较祖、母、常钱之细微变化，其字由清晰趋模糊，字划由小变大，外边由宽变狭，内边由狭变宽，径由大而小，面由平滑变凹凸，刻划角度渐无，此论当如醍醐灌顶，明者愈明。

痕迹待辨者，如光绪通宝圆规痕、道光通宝刀痕、乾隆牙雕八点细孔痕、嘉庆牙雕背四点孔痕，用途可推而论之，然工具痕迹、工艺痕迹尚且待考。

综观雕母，"雕"痕能分，时代难定，此为第一症结；雕母铸母钱、母钱修琢之工艺，雕刻工具、雕技规则、字划演变之谜题，亦需同好共发考证严谨精神，揭百年之迷局，定存世之真伪，以竟前辈之痴心，成空前绝后之举，此非我辈幸甚？更期全部珍藏早日整理成册面世，岂非盛事？

古云："余音绕梁，三月不绝"，二十八品心观时日，顿觉粉黛皆失色，字之神形之美恐难有出其右者。然此书付梓匆忙，难免纰漏，尚请同好批评指正。

愚一介微尘，充滥竽之音，强以为记，贻笑大方。

李邦兴　谨记

2019 年 10 月